ESSENTIALS of the
Clinical Mental Health Counseling Profession

Including the Key Documents of the Profession and a Career Development Guide

First Edition, February 2020

AMERICAN MENTAL HEALTH COUNSELORS ASSOCIATION

Alexandria, Virginia

CITATION GUIDE

Copyright © 2020, by the American Mental Health Counselors Association. All rights reserved. Except as permitted under the United States Copyright Act of 1976, no part of this publication may be reproduced or distributed in any form or by any means, or stored in a database or retrieval system, without the prior written permission of the publisher. However, reasonable cited excerpts are allowed.

"Essentials of the Clinical Mental Health Counseling Profession" is published by:
American Mental Health Counselors Association
107 S. West Street, Suite 779
Alexandria, VA 22314
www.amhca.org

This publication is available in paperback and e-book versions at *www.amhca.org/publications/essentials*.
First Printing: June 2019
Second Printing, First Edition: February 2020

Authors: Joel E. Miller, *Executive Director/CEO* and H. Gray Otis, *Director of Program Coordination*
Editor: Kathleen McCarthy
Cover Designer: Jim Macedone

The American Mental Health Counselors Association (AMHCA)—is committed to advancing the profession of clinical mental health counseling and improving public health. The association provides professional development, educational publications, continuing education and training career guidance, standards of practice, research, advocacy, a code of ethics, and other resources. For more information, visit *www.amhca.org*.

AMHCA Board of Directors

President: Eric T. Beeson; *President-Elect:* Angele Moss–Baker; *Past President:* H. Al Goodman; *Prior Past President:* Joseph Weeks; *Treasurer:* Donald Gilbert; *Director-at-Large:* Tony Onorato; *North Atlantic Region Director:* Ellen Papanikulaou; *Southern Region Director:* Aaron Norton; *Midwest Region Director:* James Blundo; *Western Region Director:* Karen Langer; *Graduate Student Representative:* Jennifer Reckner; *Executive Director/CEO:* Joel E. Miller

AMHCA Committee Chairs

Advancement for Clinical Practice Committee: Judith Harrington; *Ethics Committee:* Jeri Stevens; *Public Policy and Legislative Committee:* Joshua Maldonado; *State Chapter Relations Committee:* Elizabeth Nelson; *Graduate Student and Emerging Professionals Committee:* Jennifer Reckner; *Credentialing Certification Board:* Mary D. Lutzo

AMHCA Staff

Executive Director/CEO: Joel E. Miller; *Director of Operations, Finance and Membership:* Melissa McShepard; *Chief Strategic Officer and Director of Communications and State Chapter Relations:* Whitney Meyerhoeffer; *Director of the Office of Credentialing and Continuing Education:* Rebecca Gibson; *Director of Program Coordination:* H. Gray Otis

Dedicated to all those who have contributed to the profession of clinical mental health counseling.

TABLE OF CONTENTS

	Page
Introduction and Executive Summary	1
SECTION 1: The Profession of Clinical Mental Health Counseling	9
Chapter 1: What Distinguishes Licensed Clinical Mental Health Counselors From Other Mental Health Professionals?	11
Chapter 2: The Fundamental Documents of the Profession	15
Chapter 3: Career Guidance and the Phases of Clinical Mental Health Counseling Professional Development	23
Chapter 4: The History of the Clinical Mental Health Counseling Profession	41
Chapter 5: The Future of the Profession	51
SECTION 2: Professional Associations Related to Clinical Mental Health Counseling	61
Chapter 6: The Organization of the American Mental Health Counselors Association	63
Chapter 7: Other Organizations and Associations Related to Counseling	71
APPENDIXES	77
A. AMHCA's Mission and Vision	79
B. *AMHCA Standards for the Practice of Clinical Mental Health Counseling*	81
C. *AMHCA Code of Ethics*	121
D. *AMHCA Statement on Reparative or Conversion Therapy*	141
E. *AMHCA Clinical Supervision Disclosure Template*	143
F. *The AMHCA Ethical Decision-Making Model*	147
G. *The Clinical Mental Health Counselor Declaration: A Hippocratic Pledge*	149
End Note	151

Introduction and Executive Summary

The Impact of the Profession

"Deep in their roots, all flowers keep the light."
Theodore Roethke

Why is the profession of clinical mental health counseling crucial to the future of public health?

The clinical mental health counseling profession critically affects public health in the United States. Members of the profession are at the forefront of the integration of psychological wellness and holistic health. Increasingly, health care includes attention to physical health and related emotional concerns. Clinical mental health counseling is a profession of licensed specialists trained to work with individuals, couples, families, and communities to resolve complex mental disorders while promoting greater mental health and vitality. For members of the profession, "It's not just about getting better—it's about creating a better life."

Clinical Mental Health Counselors

"Essentials of the Clinical Mental Health Counseling Profession" is published by American Mental Health Counselors Association (AMHCA). "Essentials" defines this unique profession, explains its distinctive characteristics, assembles a number of the profession's fundamental documents, and provides career development guidance.

AMHCA recognizes trained clinical mental health counselor practitioners in the following categories:

- Clinical Mental Health Counseling Student (CMHC Student)—A student in a master's or doctoral educational program who provides supervised clinical mental health counseling services during internships
- Supervised Clinical Mental Health Counselor (Supervised CMHC)—A graduate of a graduate degree program who provides clinical mental health counseling services, but who is not licensed to practice without supervision
- Licensed Clinical Mental Health Counselor (LCMHC)—One who is licensed to provide clinical mental health counseling services independently, without supervision

Unless otherwise specified in this book, the acronym LCMHC is an umbrella term that also includes CMHC Students and Supervised CMHCs, both of whom provide supervised clinical mental health services. Clinical mental health counselors in all of the above categories assess or diagnose and treat mental disorders specified in the *Diagnostic and Statistical Manual of Mental Disorders (DSM–5)* of the American Psychiatric Association.

State titles for LCMHCs vary from one state to another because of licensing laws. State titles include Licensed Professional Counselor (LPC), Licensed Mental Health Counselor (LMHC), Licensed Clinical Counselor (LCC), etc. The LCMHC acronym applies to all clinical mental health counselors irrespective of their state title. Likewise, the LCMHC acronym applies regardless of the title of the individual's graduate education program. For example, LCMHCs may graduate from master's degree programs in Mental Health Counseling, Applied Psychology, or other related programs.

Distinctive Characteristics of the Profession

Those who are trained and licensed as LCMHCs possess distinguishing professional attributes. Although licensed under different state titles (e.g., Licensed Professional Counselor, Licensed Mental Health Counselor, etc.), the members of the clinical mental health counseling profession subscribe to the following:

Introduction and Executive Summary

- *Licensed to diagnose.* LCMHCs are licensed in each state to diagnose and treat mental disorders. Along with other mental health professionals, they are Primary Mental Health Care Providers who offer psychotherapy and other services for the betterment of mental and emotional well-being. Distinctively, LCMHCs focus on the total health of individuals and the growth of interpersonal relationships. This includes symptom alleviation of mental disorders while attending to the underlying causes. LCMHCs employ evidence-based, therapeutic treatment approaches that are encompassing in scope, preventive in design, and developmental in nature.

- *Holistic health focus.* Because of their holistic health integration and evidence-based treatment, LCMHCs are skilled and knowledgeable clinicians. They employ evidence-based psychotherapeutic methods and therapies such as Cognitive Behavioral Therapy. However, LCMHCs offer a range of other services, including vocational counseling, support of integrative behavioral health, couples and family counseling, etc.

- *Collaborative partnering.* Effective clinical mental health counseling integrates a collaborative effort with the client or patient and other stakeholders (such as family members, primary care providers, and policymakers). As a part of their graduate training, LCMHCs are taught to respond to cultural diversity. These mental health professionals also use the skills of leadership, advocacy, and collaboration to promote systemic changes for improved public health.

Individuals, families, communities, and our nation need effective treatment of mental health conditions along with integrated health. AMHCA, which was created in 1976 to advance the profession of clinical mental health counseling, promotes the preparation, training, and credentialing of LCMHCs. In addition, AMHCA publicly advocates for greater mental, emotional, and physiological well-being for all people.

AMHCA created this guide about the clinical mental health counseling profession to illustrate the particular benefits LCMHCs provide. Each of the other three mental health professions (Psychologists, Clinical Social Workers, and Marriage and Family Therapists) offers distinctive services, with some overlap among them. LCMHCs are distinguished by their ability to address the causes as well as the symptoms of depression, anxiety, trauma, substance use, and other mental disorders. LCMHCs effectively help individuals, families, and communities achieve richer, more fulfilling lives. Working to systematically enhance health integration, LCMHCs are on the forefront of behavioral health initiatives. The work LCMHCs do helps meet the need for effective treatment of mental health conditions along with the desirability of integrated health—a growing need that is recognized by individuals, families, communities, and our nation.

For a brief video that highlights the distinctive characteristics of Licensed Clinical Mental Health Counselors, please see *www.amhca.org/about/about-us*.

The Profession of Clinical Mental Health Counseling

Dedicated to the mental and emotional well-being of all individuals, the profession of clinical mental health counseling is composed of Licensed Clinical Mental Health Counselors (LCMHCs). LCMHCs are state-accredited to assess, diagnose, and treat mental disorders defined in the *Diagnostic and Statistical Manual of Mental Disorders* that is published by the American Psychiatric Association. However, state license titles for LCMHCs vary; they include Licensed Professional Counselors, Licensed Mental Health Counselors, Licensed Clinical Counselors, Licensed Clinical Mental Health Counselors, and other licensed designations. Regardless of license title, LCMHCs are mental health professionals recognized in all states to comprehensively treat psychological disorders and many quality-of-life challenges.

Because LCMHCs focus on mental health, they collaborate with their clients using evidence-based therapeutic approaches. They are qualified by graduate education, supervised experience, and state licensing to treat depression, anxiety, trauma, substance use behaviors, and other psychological concerns. In addition,

LCMHCs are holistically trained to address social, cultural, vocational, educational, integrated behavioral health, and physical wellness.

Members of the public, insurers, employers, federal and state agencies, and other stakeholders need information about the clinically skilled capabilities of LCMHCs. As mental health professionals, LCMHCs are rigorously qualified to provide a wide spectrum of services. To address this need for information, the American Mental Health Counselors Association (AMHCA) created, "Essentials of the Clinical Mental Health Counseling Profession" ("Essentials"). The book provides the framework for understanding the profession of clinical mental health counseling as well as the career development of LCMHCs. "Essentials" outlines the distinguishing training of LCMHCs and the applied skills they have to treat mental disorders in conjunction with other co-occurring conditions. It includes standards of training for graduate studies and postgraduate degree education, the *AMHCA Code of Ethics, The Clinical Mental Health Counselor Declaration: a Hippocratic Pledge,* advanced practice certifications for clinical specialists in one or more specializations, and other distinctive components of the profession.

In addition, "Essentials" includes several foundational documents of the clinical mental health counseling profession. These documents serve as a library of resources for all members of the profession as they advance from graduate studies through the progressive stages of their careers. "Essentials" also provides step-by-step qualification requirements that recognize professional development. For example, in addition to achieving recognition as a clinical specialist, LCMHCs can achieve AMHCA professional recognition through AMHCA's credentials and its advanced clinical practice board certifications, which are described in Chapter 3.

Purposes of "Essentials of the Clinical Mental Health Counseling Profession"

"Essentials" outlines all of the key components of the clinical mental health counseling profession and provides a unified vision for improving individual, family, and community well-being. AMHCA created "Essentials" to:

- Provide career guidance to all individuals who have chosen to become licensed in clinical mental health counseling.
- Offer information for those who may consider a vocation in clinical mental health counseling.
- Inform members of the public about the profession of clinical mental health counseling.
- Explain the distinctive characteristics of the profession to those in government, health services, and other allied associations, organizations, and stakeholders.

LCMHCs are engaged in a demanding vocation devoted to enhanced mental and emotional well-being, improved relationships, physical wellness, and enriched quality of life. This guide serves as a source document that describes the values of the profession as well as the characteristics that differentiate LMHCs from those who practice in other mental health professions.

Components of "Essentials"

A complete understanding of the profession requires a foundation of knowledge about what it means to be engaged as a Licensed Clinical Mental Health Counselor. "Essentials" provides an overview for LCMHCs to gain a greater appreciation for the vocation they have chosen.

"Essentials" is organized into two main sections, with summaries of each chapter listed below:

Introduction and Executive Summary

- ❑ SECTION 1: The Profession of Clinical Mental Health Counseling

    - o Chapter 1: What Distinguishes Licensed Clinical Mental Health Counselors From Other Mental Health Professionals? *LCMHCs are unique as Primary Mental Health Care Providers. These skilled and knowledgeable mental health professionals offer psychotherapy as well as a range of other supportive resources unique to the profession. These attributes are explained to enable members of the profession and the public to more fully appreciate the qualifications of LCMHCs.*

    - o Chapter 2: The Fundamental Documents of the Profession: *These include* The Clinical Mental Health Counselor Declaration: A Hippocratic Pledge, AMHCA Standards for the Practice of Clinical Mental Health Counseling, *and* AMHCA Code of Ethics. *In addition, AMHCA publishes two primary publications in support of these fundamental documents:* Journal of Clinical Mental Health Counseling (JMHC) *and* The Advocate Magazine.

    - o Chapter 3: Career Guidance and the Phases of Professional Development for Clinical Mental Health Counselors: *This chapter outlines each step of LCMHC professional development. Those considering the profession or who have enrolled in a graduate degree program in clinical mental health counseling will find a comprehensive roadmap of career progression especially pertinent. The career phases and the associated qualifications detailed in this chapter are compatible with, but do not supplant, any state's licensing requirements. Nevertheless, the qualifications of each career phase do confirm and recognize the individual's knowledge and understanding of the clinical mental health counseling profession.*

    - o Chapter 4: History of the Clinical Mental Health Counseling Profession: *The profession has passed a number of crucial milestones, including recognized licensing in all 50 states and the District of Columbia. Understanding this history is crucial for LCMHCs to grasp the foundations of the profession. With this historical context, they can contribute more knowledgably to present and future clinical mental health counseling initiatives.*

    - o Chapter 5: The Future of the Profession: *With an emphasis on integrated behavioral health, Licensed Clinical Mental Health Counselors are distinctively positioned to have an increasing influence in the future of mental and emotional well-being. By virtue of their education and ongoing training throughout their careers, LCMHCs continue to impact individuals, families, and communities. Additionally, the members of AMHCA's board of directors and the AMHCA staff consistently look for ways to anticipate and address future concerns and opportunities for the profession. In this chapter, a number of public health issues are identified. As part of its mission, the profession addresses these and other concerns to improve overall health and well-being.*

- ❑ SECTION 2: Professional Associations Related to Clinical Mental Health Counseling

    - o Chapter 6: The American Mental Health Counselors Association: *AMHCA is the association for the profession of clinical mental health counseling and for all LCMHCs. This chapter concisely describes the roles of the AMHCA board of directors and officers and the committees of the association; the responsibilities of the executive director/CEO; and the functions of the staff.*

    - o Chapter 7: Other Organizations and Associations Related to Counseling: *It is worthwhile to understand the key groups and alliances related to AMHCA and the other mental health professions. AMHCA and its state chapters often have opportunities to coordinate and work together with these other organizations and associations regarding issues of mutual interest.*

❑ Appendixes:

- o Appendix A: AMHCA's Mission and Vision Statements

- o Appendix B: *AMHCA Standards for the Practice of Clinical Mental Health Counseling: These standards of practice provide a guide to the breadth and depth of clinical mental health counseling. They include the knowledge and skills of each area of specialized focus within the profession.* AMHCA Standards *was first published in 1979, three years after AMHCA was established, and is continuously updated to reflect the latest scientific advancements in psychology, neuroscience, supervision standards, and evidence-based treatment modalities.*

- o Appendix C: *AMHCA Code of Ethics: Because it is written specifically for LCMHCs as well as CMHC Students and Supervised CMHCs, the* AMHCA Code of Ethics *addresses concerns pertaining to the practice of clinical mental health counseling. Members of the profession should adhere to the* AMHCA Code of Ethics, *regardless of other codes of ethics that may be applicable to them. The* Code of Ethics *is updated as needed to discuss issues of vital importance to the public, legislative bodies, and other interested parties.*

- o Appendix D: *AMHCA Statement on Reparative or Conversion Therapy: In 2014, the AMHCA board of directors issued a formal statement regarding reparative or conversion therapy. These types of therapeutic approaches are not considered ethically valid.*

- o Appendix E: *AMHCA Clinical Supervision Disclosure Template: LCMHCs who are supervisors should consider specific ethical questions. The* AMHCA Clinical Supervision Disclosure Template *provides a model for supervision.*

- o Appendix F: The AMHCA Ethical Decision-Making Model: *Having a systematic approach is helpful when considering ethical concerns.* The AMHCA Ethical Decision-Making Model *is a valid means of addressing these issues.*

- o Appendix G: *The Clinical Mental Health Declaration: A Hippocratic Pledge*

The Necessity for the Profession of Clinical Mental Health Counseling

Studies show that people need access to mental health professionals to resolve a wide variety of mental disorders and other emotional concerns. Licensed Clinical Mental Health Counselors are increasingly playing a vital role in the wellness of communities and in the interests of the nation's health because they are Primary Mental Health Care Providers with a focus on integrated behavioral health.

"Essentials" illustrates how LCMHCs can be highly effective in the treatment of psychological concerns. While psychiatry, neuroscience, and psychopharmacology have contributed to improved conditions for many patients, LCMHCs, as qualified psychotherapy specialists, have immense impact in actually resolving the underlying causes of disorder symptoms. By resolving these underlying causes, LCMHCs positively impact the growing concerns about substance use and opioids, the swelling rates of PTSD diagnoses, the impact on families, the burden that untreated mental disorders place on medical resources, and other behavioral health issues. Even in the context of depression and anxiety, prescribed psychotropic medications help to lessen symptoms, but they cannot be depended on to address the underlying causes.

More and more, successful resolution of mental health disorders depends on effective, evidence-based clinical mental health counseling. LCMHCs are trained to use a range of treatment modalities including psychotherapeutic interventions, couples and family counseling, substance use and co-occurring disorders treatment, vocational rehabilitation, group counseling work, etc. In addition to being trained to work in concert with medical specialists, including primary care physicians, they are positioned to participate on integrated treatment teams. With their education in neuroscience and psychotropic medications, their breadth of academic, developmental, and clinical knowledge makes them particularly effective integrated behavioral health practitioners.

Their focused education on clinical mental health treatment—along with their training, applied skills, and holistic health perspective—puts LCMHCs on the leading edge of treatment effectiveness as Primary Mental Health Care Providers. As the public's awareness of their abilities and their professional skills grows, they will be sought out even more to provide successful and enduring patient outcomes.

"Essentials of the Clinical Mental Health Counseling Profession" is a living document that AMHCA will update regularly. Readers are encouraged to contribute their ideas for future updates by using the comment box on the "Essentials" page at *www.amhca.org/publications/essentials*.

Section 1

THE PROFESSION OF CLINICAL MENTAL HEALTH COUNSELING

CHAPTER 1

What Distinguishes Licensed Clinical Mental Health Counselors From Other Mental Health Professionals?

Appreciating the Characteristics and Attributes of the Profession

"Quality tends to fan out like waves."
Robert M. Pirsig

What do Clinical Mental Health Counselors offer as Primary Mental Health Care Providers?

Four nationally recognized mental health professions train individuals to become licensed and qualified to offer mental health therapy (or psychotherapy):

- Mental Health Counseling: Licensed Clinical Mental Health Counselor (LCMHC)
- Psychology: Licensed Clinical or Counseling Psychologist (Licensed Psychologist)
- Social Work: Licensed Clinical Social Worker (LCSW)
- Marriage and Family Therapy: Licensed Marriage and Family Therapist (LMFT)

License titles for all these mental health professions can vary from state-to-state. LCMHCs are licensed by a variety of titles. However, they all belong to the historically established profession of clinical mental health counseling that dates back to 1976. AMHCA refers to all mental health counselors who are licensed to clinically diagnose and treat mental disorders as Licensed Clinical Mental Health Counselors, or LCMHCs. As noted on page 2, the acronym LCMHC is used in the body of this book to also refer to CMHC Students and Supervised CMHCs, who are seeking full licensure.

LCMHCs are uniquely educated and licensed in ways that make them distinct from the other mental health professions. Like members of the other three professions, LCMHCs have either a master's or doctoral degree. In their graduate studies, they become qualified in psychopathology and in the diagnosis and treatment of psychological disorders. Philosophically, they are trained to be holistic and strength-based in working with individuals, couples, families, and groups. In addition, they strive to focus on treating both the symptoms and causes of mental and emotional concerns.

Graduate education in clinical mental health counseling encompasses several specialized courses of study that may not be included in the other mental health professions. A typical, accredited master's degree program in clinical mental health counseling covers the following subjects:

- Professional counseling orientation and ethical practice
- Social and cultural diversity and cultural factors relevant to clinical mental health counseling
- Human growth and development
- Counseling and helping relationships
- Ethics and legal considerations specific to clinical mental health counseling
- Principles, models, and documentation formats of biopsychosocial case conceptualization and treatment planning
- The neurobiological and medical foundation of mental health disorders
- The etiology of addiction and co-occurring mental disorders
- Theories and models related to clinical mental health counseling
- Intake interview, mental status evaluation, biopsychosocial history, mental health history, and psychological assessment for treatment planning and caseload management
- Diagnostic process, including differential diagnosis and the use of current diagnostic classification systems, including the *Diagnostic and Statistical Manual of Mental Disorders (DSM)* and the *International Classification of Diseases* (ICD)
- Group counseling and group work

Chapter 1: What Distinguishes LCMHCs From Other Mental Health Professionals?

- ❑ Individual counseling and psychotherapy for children, adolescents, and adults of all ages
- ❑ Couples and family counseling
- ❑ Research and program evaluation
- ❑ Career development
- ❑ Mental health assessment test instruments that are specific to scope of practice
- ❑ Etiology, nomenclature, treatment, referral, and prevention of mental and emotional disorders
- ❑ Mental health service delivery modalities within the continuum of care, such as inpatient, outpatient, partial treatment, aftercare, and mental health counseling services networks
- ❑ Record keeping, comprehensive case documentation, third-party reimbursement, and other practice and management issues in clinical mental health counseling
- ❑ The assessment and treatment of substance use disorders and co-occurring disorders to include neurological, medical, and physiological considerations
- ❑ Crisis and trauma mental health diagnoses and trauma-informed care
- ❑ Psychopharmacological medication classifications, indications, and contraindications of commonly prescribed medications, and appropriate medical referral and consultation
- ❑ Impact of biological and neurological mechanisms on mental health
- ❑ Collaboration with integrated behavioral health care professionals and medical specialists
- ❑ Interventions for prevention and treatment of a broad range of mental health issues
- ❑ Strategies to advocate for persons with mental health issues

These topics of instruction are integrated into clinical mental health counseling master's degree programs. These programs are commonly state mandated to be not less than 60 semester hours of instruction.

LCMHCs may continue their education. Doctoral students complete all the above master's degree studies and then typically go on to earn a PhD or EdD doctorate from an accredited program in Counselor Education and Supervision or Counseling Education. Their coursework includes additional education in clinical mental health counseling and advanced research, culminating in writing a doctoral dissertation. Often, these highly qualified graduates focus on teaching and research in universities with master's degree programs in clinical mental health counseling.

Education in clinical mental health counseling also addresses several emerging public health concerns. Three of these crucial matters are addressed throughout educational programs:

1. *Trauma-informed care.* Increasing attention has been placed on the need for the effective treatment of trauma disorders and chronic anxiety. Students in mental health counseling educational programs are trained to diagnose and treat these conditions with established, evidence-based psychotherapeutic approaches.

2. *Substance use and co-morbid disorders, with added attention to other behavioral compulsions.* Students in mental health counseling programs have been historically trained to deal with addictions and the co-occurring disorders that accompany dependence on alcohol, drugs, or prescribed medications. Increasingly, this cluster of public health concerns also address disorders such as gambling, eating disorders, self-harm, and other compulsive behaviors.

3. *Integrated behavioral health.* Early in the genesis of the profession of clinical mental health counseling, educational coursework reflected an awareness of the need to address the whole person. The link between the practice of medicine and mental health therapy has been demonstrated in numerous studies. Students in mental health counseling programs understand the importance of whole-health

assessment as well as the growing requirement for integrated behavioral health collaboration with primary care providers and other medical professionals.

Before graduating, clinical mental health counseling students—both master's degree and doctoral degree candidates—must complete an applied practicum or internship working with clients or patients under the supervision of seasoned mental health professionals. Only after they have demonstrated the ability to provide mental health counseling in a clinical setting can they be approved to graduate by their supervisors and their faculty.

Although Clinical Mental Health Counselors qualify for initial state licensure when they graduate, they must then meet the requirements to become fully licensed. For at least two years, they work under the direction of a licensed qualified supervisor while accumulating a required minimum of 3,000 hours of experience. During this time, they are employed in various settings; they continue their education through courses, seminars, or conferences; and they prepare to pass a national qualification examination. When they meet all of the licensing requirements, they apply for full licensure.

LCMHCs offer a comprehensive spectrum of therapeutic services as Primary Mental Health Care Providers. Their unique combination of holistic focus, rigorous training, and advanced practice experience prepares them for careers that promote public health. Most LCMHCs eventually become specialized in one or more specialty areas of practice. These counseling specializations include children and adolescents, trauma resolution, couples and family, compulsive behaviors or substance use recovery, domestic violence, gerontology, integrated behavioral health counseling in medical settings, and many other subspecialties. Working in a variety of settings and serving diverse populations with increasingly complex health concerns, LCMHCs are among the most knowledgeable and skilled mental health professionals because they typically have more coursework and experience focused directly on therapeutic clinical work.

CHAPTER 2

The Fundamental Documents of the Profession

The Central Values and Ideals
of Clinical Mental Health Counseling

"The facts are always friendly, every bit of evidence one can acquire, in any area, leads one that much closer to what is true."

Carl Rogers, PhD

How do the fundamental documents of the profession apply to the practice of Clinical Mental Health Counseling?

All professions have principal documents that describe the basic functions of professional conduct. The American Mental Health Counselors Association (AMHCA) has published the foundational documents for Clinical Mental Health Counseling Students (CMHC Students), Supervised Clinical Mental Health Counselors (Supervised CMHCs), and Licensed Clinical Mental Health Counselors (LCMHCs):

- *The Clinical Mental Health Counselor Declaration: A Hippocratic Pledge* (see page 18 and Appendix G, on page 149): The *AMHCA Declaration* was developed as an adjunct to the *AMHCA Code of Ethics*. This one-page, public declaration is a commitment of LCMHCs to serve others with honor and integrity.

- *AMHCA Standards for the Practice of Clinical Mental Health Counseling (Appendix B)*: *AMHCA Standards* serves as a framework of specific knowledge and skills criteria for the profession of clinical mental health counseling.

- *AMHCA Code of Ethics (Appendix C)*: The *AMHCA Code of Ethics* is a detailed description of applied ethical practice that specifically addresses issues of concerns for CMHC Students, Supervised CMHCs, and LCMHCs.

In support of the fundamental documents above, AMHCA publishes the *Journal of Clinical Mental Health Counseling (JMHC)*, *The Advocate Magazine*, Practice Guidelines, and Position Papers. AMHCA also promotes continuing education through professional development training courses, webinars, and conferences.

Members of the association have access to professional development training and to each of these publications. The publications are also available to individuals who are not AMHCA members for research or other studies.

The *Journal* is a peer-reviewed publication that has been published since 1978. It addresses all aspects of practice, theory, professionalism, research, and neurocounseling related to the clinical mental health counseling profession. *The Advocate Magazine* provides legislative advocacy updates, and articles relevant to practice issues for LCMHCs—such as ways to protect themselves from potentially violent clients, working in integrated care settings, and understanding the neurobiology of trauma. Every issue also includes columns by AMHCA's president and its executive director/CEO.

What Is *The Clinical Mental Health Counselor Declaration*, and How Does It Apply to the Practice of Mental Health Counseling?

For centuries, medical professionals have been bound by the Hippocratic Oath or other pledges of fidelity to their profession and to their patients. These pledges are statements for individual practitioners to openly affirm their commitment to serve with care and integrity. Physicians are also required to adhere to standards of ethical conduct. Likewise, mental health professionals have codes of ethics that oblige them to be accountable to the public and answerable to state boards of licensure.

The Clinical Mental Health Counselor Declaration reflects the *AMHCA Code of Ethics*. It is a public affirmation of adherence to the comprehensive provisions of the *AMHCA Code of Ethics*. All LCMHCs are encouraged to adhere to the values and ethics embodied in *The AMHCA Declaration*. All those who seek AMHCA qualifications and certifications (see Chapter 3) as part of their career advancement and recognition are presumed to understand and apply the components of *The Clinical Mental Health Counselor Declaration*.

The AMHCA Declaration serves as a concise public statement of professional standards, values, and ideals. It is a voluntary pronouncement. If they desire, LCMHCs are encouraged to display *The AMHCA Declaration* in their office. It may also be used at graduations or for other appropriate occasions.

The Clinical Mental Health Counselor Declaration follows and is available at *www.amhca.org/publications/declaration*. A version suitable for framing is in Appendix G on page 150.

The Clinical Mental Health Counselor Declaration
A Hippocratic Pledge

Clinical Mental Health Counselors advocate for the well-being of individuals, families, and communities. They are highly trained and qualified to provide comprehensive assessment, diagnosis, and treatment of mental health disorders as well as barriers to quality of life. Members of the profession also integrate mental health with social, cultural, vocational, educational, and physical wellness.

As a Clinical Mental Health Counselor:

I pledge to dedicate my professional life to the service of humanity;

My first consideration will be to improve the mental, emotional, and relational well-being of those within my care, their families, and the community at large;

I will engage in my profession with integrity and in keeping with codes of ethics, laws, and the best practices of Clinical Mental Health Counseling;

I will maintain the utmost respect for each individual and will honor their autonomy, dignity, and self-determination;

I will respect the confidences that are disclosed to me, in accordance with relevant laws and codes of ethics;

I will recognize and address presumptions related to gender, age, race, ethnic origin, sexual orientation, disease, ability level, creed, nationality, or any other factors so they will not interfere with my duties;

I will honor my professional capabilities, so that even under threat, I will not violate human rights or civil liberties;

I will share my professional knowledge and work in partnership with other health professionals;

I will extend fitting respect and gratitude to my teachers, colleagues, and students;

I will use my knowledge, skills, and experiences to prepare the next generation of Clinical Mental Health Counselors;

I will attend to my own well-being, my physical wellness, and my personal relationships;

I will accept my lifelong obligation to improve my professional capabilities in order to provide the highest standard of care; and

As a Clinical Mental Health Counselor, I will advocate for the betterment of others and for the advancement of health and well-being.

I make this declaration solemnly, freely, and on my honor.

© 2020 AMHCA / *The Clinical Mental Health Declaration* was developed by the board of directors of the American Mental Health Counselors Association. Permission is granted to appropriately reproduce, display, and distribute this declaration.

How Are the Criteria of the *AMHCA Standards* Employed?

AMHCA Standards for the Practice of Clinical Mental Counseling specifies the established benchmarks of practice for Licensed Clinical Mental Health Counselors (LCMHCs). Created by the American Mental Health Counselors Association (AMHCA), *AMHCA Standards* identifies and describes norms within the profession for education, training, and application.

The standards spelled out in this important document have served as the foundation of the profession since 1979 when they were first adopted. *AMHCA Standards* has been periodically revised and extended as the profession developed. In the past, the explicit requirements for practice, education, and supervision were used to validate clinical mental health counselor qualifications as one of the four recognized mental health professions (the other three are psychology, social work, and marriage and family therapy).

The National Academy of Medicine (formerly the Institute of Medicine) in its 2010 report cited the *AMHCA Standards* as justification for LCMHC qualification and eligibility for federal employment and reimbursement. It reported: "Independent practice of mental health counselors for TRICARE in the circumstances in which their education, licensure, and clinical experience have helped to prepare them to diagnose, and where appropriate, treat conditions in the beneficiary population" ("Provision of Mental Health Counseling Services Under TRICARE," Chapter 6, page 207, at *bit.ly/2qqYyxP*.

AMHCA Standards for the Practice of Clinical Mental Health Counseling is a living document that is updated on a continuing basis to meet the needs of the public and the profession. In addition to standards of practice, it includes training and supervision standards.

Of special note are the specific clinical mental health counseling specialist knowledges and skills. The need is expanding for mental health professionals who have advanced, postgraduate training and experience in treating populations with special needs. AMHCA's Advancement for Clinical Practice Committee has been at the forefront of identifying the knowledge and skills required for LCMHCs to become specialists. Examples of areas of clinical specialization include:

- Aging and Older Adults Standards and Competencies
- Biological Bases of Behavior
- Child and Adolescent Standards and Competencies
- Integrated Behavioral Health Care Counseling
- Specialized Clinical Assessment
- Substance Use Disorders and Co-occurring Disorders
- Technology Supported Counseling and Communications (TSCC)
- Trauma-Informed Care

Currently the committee is working on including Military Counseling, Couples and Family Counseling, and Developmental and Learning Disabilities Counseling.

AMHCA Standards for the Practice of Clinical Mental Health Counseling has been revised several times. Additionally, the AMHCA Advancement for Clinical Practice Committee constantly reviews and updates *AMHCA Standards* as appropriate.

The Committee continues to establish new standards for inclusion. The unabridged version of *AMHCA Standards for the Practice of Clinical Mental Health Counseling* appears in Appendix B and is downloadable at no cost from *www.amhca.org/publications/standards*.

How Is the *AMHCA Code of Ethics* Distinctive for the Profession?

Created by the American Mental Health Counselors Association (AMHCA), the *AMHCA Code of Ethics* focuses on the specific requirements for the ethical practice for Clinical Mental Health Counseling Students (CMHC Students), Supervised Clinical Mental Health Counselors (Supervised CMHCs), and Licensed Clinical Mental Health Counselors (LCMHCs). All recognized professions have codes of ethics to guide the conduct of practice in order to ensure the safety of those served.

Continuously updated to meet the needs of changing circumstances, the *AMHCA Code of Ethics* addresses the crucial concerns of the profession. The association's Ethics Committee, a standing committee, reviews, revises, and adds to the *AMHCA Code of Ethics* in keeping with current standards of practice and applicable ethical standards. This committee serves as a conduit for ethical questions. In this never-ending process, the committee members solicit feedback from all stakeholders. They also refer to other codes of ethics in order to be in harmony with the mental health professions including psychology, social work, marriage and family therapy, etc. Nevertheless, the *AMHCA Code of Ethics* reflects the unique needs of the clinical mental health counseling profession.

With frequent updates, the *Code of Ethics* is often at the forefront of articulating developments in counseling and psychotherapy. For example, technology advances in tele-health (distance counseling) prompted an addition to the *Code of Ethics* to address the concerns of the public and the profession.

AMHCA Code of Ethics has been compared favorably in doctoral research to the codes of ethics of the other mental health professions. All members of AMHCA are required to comply with the *AMHCA Code of Ethics,* which has been adopted by some states as the standard of ethical practice. Whether or not an individual is bound by this *Code of Ethics*, all CMHC Students, Supervised CMHCs, and LCMHCs ethically should understand and act in accordance with it. *AMHCA Code of Ethics* is an essential component of practicing clinical mental health counseling with professionalism and integrity. It is required study for AMHCA qualifications and certifications.

In summation, *AMHCA Code of Ethics* offers guidelines for value-directed conduct. While ethical guidance for the practice of clinical mental health counseling is its primary purpose, it is also intended to prompt contemplation about ethical reasoning and practice. Ethics are considered in ongoing self-deliberation and in discussions with other mental health professionals.

Using the most frequently asked ethics questions that mental health counselors have submitted, AMHCA's Ethics Committee has compiled the questions and the Committee's answers into an online resource for counselors. Anyone (whether or not a member of AMHCA) can submit a question for consideration. To review the questions and answers, go to "Frequently Asked Questions on Ethics" at *www.amhca.org/publications/ethics/ethicsfaq.*

The unabridged version of *AMHCA Code of Ethics* appears in Appendix C, and it is available online at *www.amhca.org/publications/ethics.*

How Does AMHCA's *Journal* Support AMHCA's Mission to Advance the Clinical Mental Health Counseling Profession?

AMHCA's leading periodical publication, the *Journal of Mental Health Counseling* is a peer-reviewed scholarly journal that has been published since 1978. "*JMHC* is known for high-quality articles that further the scientific knowledge base, define and enhance the profession, and speak to clinicians, educators, and students," said Dr. Quinn Pearson, editor of *JMHC* from 2011-2014.

JMHC articles address all aspects of practice, theory, professionalism, research, and neurocounseling related to the clinical mental health counseling profession. *JMHC* is divided into five sections:

- *Practice:* Licensed Clinical Mental Health Counselors (LCMHCs) work in a variety of clinical settings with diverse client populations. This section emphasizes cutting-edge strategies and techniques as well as innovative applications of established clinical practices. Articles provide critical analyses of the existing literature and descriptive application of clinical approaches, strategies, and techniques.

- *Theory.* Explanations of theoretical constructs and their application in clinical mental health practice are the emphasis of this section. Theoretical articles must be well grounded in the existing conceptual and empirical literature, delineate implications for practice, and provide illustrative applications (e.g., case studies).

- *Professional Exchange.* This section allows for dialogue among LCMHCs regarding dilemmas, challenges, divergent perspectives, and other emergent topics relevant to clinical mental health counseling.

- *Research.* This section addresses empirically supported best practices, evidenced-based approaches, and new developments in clinical mental health counseling. Articles include implications for professional mental health counseling practice and future research.

- *Neurocounseling.* The goal of the Neurocounseling section is to increase scholarship related to neurocounseling by providing a dedicated space for academic discourse. This section provides LCMHCs with an opportunity to enhance clinical training and practice in a brain-based era of mental health and wellness. In order to accomplish this goal, the section has several objectives:
    - Provide a dedicated space for neuroscience manuscripts in the counseling field.
    - Identify clinical outcomes in an era of neuroscience.
    - Generate and evaluate new theories and techniques of clinical mental health counseling grounded in neuroscience principles.
    - Replicate and validate existing psychotherapy research within a counseling framework.
    - Increase exposure to the Research Domain Criteria in the counseling field.
    - Create an independent body of neurocounseling literature.

Through the five sections of the *JMHC*, the *Journal* is able to increase its focus on advanced practice (and current practice) as well as inform and enhance the other related cornerstone documents and programs on professional development. The *Journal* has an eye on expanding into new areas such as new and emerging interventions, cutting-edge counseling approaches, innovative training in clinical mental health counseling, advanced assessment and diagnosis, supervision, wellness-based counseling, and diversity within clinical mental health counseling.

AMHCA members have free access to all electronic issues of AMHCA's *Journal* and unlimited downloads. The *Journal* is available in a fully searchable database-driven format that can be found at *www.amhca.org/publications/jmhc*.

CHAPTER 3

Career Guidance and the Phases of Professional Development for Licensed Clinical Mental Health Counselors

Advancement Within the Profession of
Clinical Mental Health Counseling

*"Success is not the key to happiness. Happiness is the key to success.
If you love what you are doing, you will be successful."*

Albert Schweitzer

How to create a plan for dynamic professional development

The American Mental Health Counselors Association (AMHCA) was the first association to recognize advanced professional expertise in clinical mental health counseling. AMHCA leaders believe that highly developed skills are in increasing demand. Both the public and insurance providers are looking for Licensed Clinical Mental Health Counselors (LCMHCs) who have acquired cutting-edge training and clinical abilities. As noted on page 2, the acronym LCMHC is used in the body of this book to also refer to CMHC Students and Supervised CMHCs, who are seeking full licensure.

The first AMHCA credential that recognized advanced practice and specialist skills was the AMHCA *Diplomate and Clinical Mental Health Specialist (Diplomate or DCMHS)*. It was created to enhance the stature of individual LCMHCs and in turn, increase the prominence of the clinical mental health counseling profession. After two years of research and development, the DCMHS was approved in 2011 by the AMHCA board of directors. In 2019, the board approved a new, five-phase career development path that replaces the DCMHS with three advanced certifications.

The Five Phases of Professional Development for a Career in Clinical Mental Health Counseling

There are five career phases in the clinical mental health counseling profession. For those who desire professional development in a clinical mental health counseling career, these phases include:

- *Phase 1*—Clinical Mental Health Counseling Student (CMHC Student):

    A student enrolled in a master's or doctoral degree program related to mental health counseling

- *Phase 2*—Supervised Clinical Mental Health Counselor (Supervised CMHC):

    A graduate of a master's degree program or doctoral degree program who provides clinical mental health counseling services, but who may only practice under supervision

- *Phase 3*—Licensed Clinical Mental Health Counselor (Licensed CMHC):

    An individual who is licensed to provide clinical mental health counseling services and to practice independently, without supervision

- *Phase 4*—LCMHC Certified in Clinical Mental Health Counseling Advanced Practice:

    This phase includes individuals who are licensed to provide clinical mental health counseling services and who have professional expertise beyond full licensure to practice independently. The three Phase 4 advanced practitioner certifications that are available are listed on page 26.

- *Phase 5*—LCMHC Recognized for Exceptional Service to the Profession:

    Recognized achievement by the AMHCA board of directors for exceptional service to the profession

The roadmap for professional development in clinical mental health counseling was established to enable each individual to reach the highest standards of professional expertise. This step-by-step approach to career advancement is crucial to progressing in the profession.

AMHCA Career Development Credentialing (Phases 1–3) and Board Certification (Phases 4–5) Program

To recognize achievement at every level of career progression in the field of clinical mental health counseling, AMHCA has developed a set of requirements for each of the career phases listed above. The first three phases make up the initial credentialing of CMHC Students, Supervised CMHCs, and Licensed CMHCs. Phases 4 and 5 represent the advanced board certifications of an LCMHC career.

AMHCA members who fulfill the requirements for any phase earn a certificate and a digital badge that confirm they have met the qualifications for that credential or board certification. Digital badges are an electronic "logo" of the certification that may be attached to correspondence, web pages, etc.

The requirements for each of these certifications and board credentials are listed on the following pages. They can also be found at *www.amhca.org/career/credential*.

Initial AMHCA Credentialing for a Clinical Mental Health Counselor

Phases 1, 2, and 3 are the initial phases of a clinical mental health counseling career. Each phase of career development corresponds to a related AMHCA certification.

- ❑ *Phase 1 credentialing:* AMHCA Clinical Mental Health Counseling Student Credential (CMHC Student Credential)

    Those enrolled in a master's degree program related to mental health counseling can complete the requirements for the Clinical Mental Health Counseling Student Credential. These students will be welcomed into the career when they become a student member of AMHCA and acknowledge their commitment to the profession.

- ❑ *Phase 2 credentialing:* AMHCA Supervised Clinical Mental Health Counselor Credential (Supervised CMHC Credential)

    Graduates of mental health counseling related master's degree programs who have completed the requirements to obtain initial state licensure can also complete the requirements for the Supervised Clinical Mental Health Counselor Credential. In addition to joining AMHCA as an Emerging Professional Member, these individuals will demonstrate a basic knowledge of the profession and its foundational documents.

- ❑ *Phase 3 credentialing:* AMHCA Independent Clinical Mental Health Counselor Credential (Independent CMHC Credential)

    Individuals who have been licensed in their state for independent practice without supervision can complete the requirements to earn the Independent CMHC Credential. The qualification will attest that the individual is aware of the professional requirements of *AMHCA Standards for the Practice of Clinical Mental Health Counseling, AMHCA Code of Ethics,* and *The Clinical Mental Health Counselor Declaration.* These individuals appreciate that it is crucial for them to apply these concepts throughout their careers. Finally, they recognize the need for continuing development of professional expertise as their career advances.

Advanced AMHCA Board Certification for a Clinical Mental Health Counselor

For fully licensed LCMHCs, AMHCA offers advanced credentialing certifications. The establishment of board certification provides added professional credibility. These credentialing certifications give evidence of increasing professional competence and expertise that can convey to clients that an LCMHC holds independently recognized competencies.

Phase 4 Board Certifications

All three of the Phase 4 board certifications are evaluated and approved by the AMHCA Credentialing Certification Board. This board is composed of seasoned licensed mental health professionals, at least three of whom independently assess every application and determine if the applicant meets all of the criteria. Qualified applicants receive an AMHCA certificate and may use the corresponding digital badge. The Phase 4 advanced certifications include:

- *Phase 4a board certification:* AMHCA Clinical Mental Health Counseling Specialist (CMHC Specialist), board-certified in one or more specialization areas, e.g., Trauma (CMHC Specialist–Trauma)

   The designation as an AMHCA Clinical Mental Health Counseling Specialist is earned by LCMHCs who have achieved professional expertise in one or more specializations (e.g., CMHC Specialist in Trauma, CMHC Specialist in Substance Use Disorders and Co-occurring Disorders, etc.). Other specializations will be added by AMHCA as the need for additional specialist areas arises.

   All members of the profession are encouraged to obtain one or more specializations. To become a CMHC Specialist, candidates must have advanced postgraduate education that specifically addresses their qualifications in the specialist area and applicable clinical experience. More information about becoming a CMHC Specialist as well as the online electronic application can be found at *www.amhca.org/career/credential/apply*.

- *Phase 4b board certification:* AMHCA Clinical Mental Health Counseling Diplomate (CMHC Diplomate), board-certified in advanced clinical mental health counseling practice

   The AMHCA Clinical Mental Health Counseling Diplomate, board-certified in advanced clinical mental health counseling practice, signifies that an LCMHC has attained advanced standing in the profession. This standing is attested to by experience, accomplishments, and by service to the profession. CMHC Diplomates are LCMHCs who have achieved a high level of general clinical practice. Full requirements for the CMHC Diplomate are available online at *www.amhca.org/career/credential/apply/diplomate*.

- *Phase 4c board certification:* AMHCA Clinical Mental Health Counseling Fellow (CMHC Fellow), board-certified in clinical mental health counseling education and research

   The AMHCA Clinical Mental Health Counseling Fellow, board-certified in clinical mental health counseling education and research, signifies that an LCMHC has attained advanced standing as an educator and/or researcher. Much like the CMHC Diplomate, the standing of CMHC Fellow is attested to by experience, accomplishments, and by service to the profession, with a focus on academic research and/or teaching. The CMHC Fellow designates LCMHCs who have achieved the highest standards of education and research specifically in the profession of clinical mental health counseling. Full requirements for the CMHC Fellow are available online at *www.amhca.org/career/credential/apply/fellow*.

Chapter 3: Career Guidance and the Phases of Professional Development for LCMHCs

Phase 5 Board Certification

- *Phase 5 board certification:* AMHCA Clinical Mental Health Counseling Laureate (CMHC Laureate), board-certified for exceptional service to the profession

    The CMHC Laureate is awarded for contributions to the profession that are recognized by the board of directors. Individuals with more than 10 years of full licensure are eligible to be nominated for this award.

The AMHCA Credentialing (Phases 1–3) and Board Certification (Phases 4–5) program is summarized in the chart on the next page.

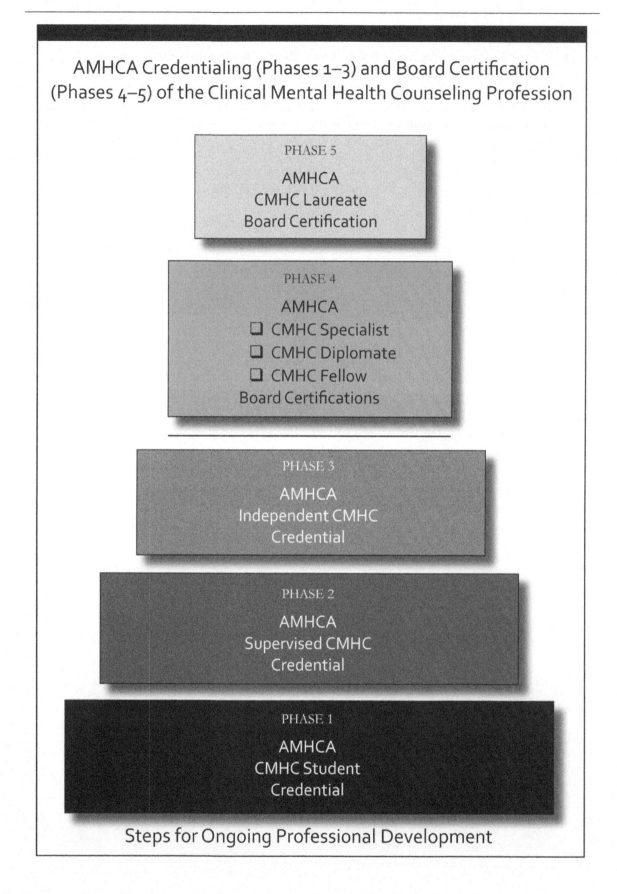

Chapter 3: Career Guidance and the Phases of Professional Development for LCMHCs

Credentialing (Phases 1–3) and Board Certification (Phases 4–5) for the Career Development of Clinical Mental Health Counselors

The chart on the previous page illustrates a general trajectory for a long and fruitful career as a Clinical Mental Health Counselor. AMHCA developed and monitors career credentialing and board certification.

In the following pages, the five phases of career development are described along with the AMHCA-related credentials to recognize career advancement. The requirements for each of the qualifications and certifications are also listed. With each of these certifications, successful applicants will be awarded a certificate and a corresponding digital badge.

You can apply for an AMHCA credential or board certification at any level at which you qualify. For instance, a seasoned professional with eight years of fully licensed service could complete the requirements for Phase 3 credentialing or Phase 4 board certification, even though they were not previously credentialed at Phase 1 or Phase 2.

Phase 1—Clinical Mental Health Counseling Student (CMHC Student)

Individuals who are enrolled in a regionally accredited clinical mental health counseling related graduate program.

Phase 1 credentialing:

AMHCA Clinical Mental Health Counseling Student Credential (CMHC Student Credential)

Requirements:

Join AMHCA as a Student Member.

Review all of the chapters in the "Essentials of the Clinical Mental Health Counseling Profession."

1. Attest to having read *The Clinical Mental Health Counselor Declaration* and to having discussed what it means to you with at least one other clinical mental health counseling student.

2. Complete the online application for the credential. There is no fee to earn the CMHC Student Credential.

Successful applicants will be awarded a PDF AMHCA certificate and will be allowed to display the corresponding digital badge. They may identify themselves as a credentialed "AMHCA Clinical Mental Health Counseling Student" or "CMHC Student."

Phase 2—Supervised Clinical Mental Health Counselor (Supervised CMHC)

Individuals who have completed initial state licensing and are under supervision after earning a master's degree in clinical mental health counseling. Supervised CMHCs work to complete the state licensing requirements for independent practice.

Phase 2 credentialing:

AMHCA Supervised Clinical Mental Health Counselor Credential (Supervised CMHC Credential)

Requirements:
Join AMHCA as an Emerging Professional Member.
Review all of the chapters in "The Essentials of the Clinical Mental Health Counseling Profession." 1. Attest to having completed an open-book, multiple-choice examination covering: ❏ *The Clinical Mental Health Counselor Declaration* ❏ Phases of Career Development ❏ History of the Profession ❏ *AMHCA Standards for the Practice of Clinical Mental Health Counseling* ❏ *AMHCA Code of Ethics* This exam will be available online and self-scored. 2. Complete the online application and pay the application processing fee for the Supervised CMHC Credential. Successful applicants will be awarded a PDF AMHCA certificate and will be allowed to display the corresponding digital badge. They may identify themselves as a credentialed "AMHCA Supervised Clinical Mental Health Counselor" or "Supervised CMHC."

Chapter 3: Career Guidance and the Phases of Professional Development for LCMHCs

Phase 3—Licensed Clinical Mental Health Counselor (Licensed CMHC)

Individuals who have completed all of the licensing requirements as defined by the respective state and awarded the license to practice independently.

	*Phase 3 credentialing:* AMHCA Independent Clinical Mental Health Counselor Credential (Independent CMHC Credential)
Requirements:	
Join AMHCA as a Clinical Member.	
Complete all of the following requirements: 1. If not previously accomplished, review all chapters in "Essentials" and complete the open-book, multiple-choice examination required in Phase 2 Certification. This exam will be available online and self-scored. 2. Attest to having a discussion with an LCMHC regarding your thoughts on, "What does means to me to be a Clinical Mental Health Counselor who is licensed to practice independently?" 3. On the application, list the state that issued your license, the title of the license to practice independently (e.g. Licensed Mental Health Counselor, Licensed Professional Counselor, etc.), and the license identification number. 4. Complete the online application and pay the application processing fee for the Independent CMHC Credential. Successful applicants will be awarded a PDF AMHCA certificate and will be allowed to display the corresponding digital badge. They may identify themselves as a credentialed "AMHCA Independent Clinical Mental Health Counselor" or "Independent CMHC."	

Phase 4—Advanced Professional Board Certifications

There are three distinctly separate Phase 4—Advanced Professional Board Certifications. AMHCA members have the opportunity to be recognized in one or more areas of developed expertise. There is no order of precedence for these certifications.

For those who have previously earned the AMHCA Diplomate and Clinical Mental Health Specialist (DCMHS): These individuals retain this distinction and may continue to use this designation. However, they are recognized by AMHCA as having qualified for board certification as both an "AMHCA Clinical Mental Health Counseling Specialist" or "CMHC Specialist" (e.g., "CMHC Specialist–Trauma") and also as an "AMHCA Clinical Mental Health Counseling Diplomate" or "CMHC Diplomate." In addition, it is appropriate for these individuals to display the corresponding digital badges.

The Advanced Professional Certifications are awarded by AMHCA only to Clinical Mental Health Counselors who are licensed to practice independently in their respective state. Qualified individuals may apply for one or more of the three separate and distinct board certifications. Every application is reviewed independently by at least three members of the AMHCA Credentialing Certification Board. All applicants must be an AMHCA Clinical Member in good standing. Applicants who have not previously completed the requirement for Phase 2 and Phase 3 Certification are required to review all of the chapters in "Essentials of the Clinical Mental Health Counseling Profession."

In addition to the requirements for the AMHCA advanced board certifications listed here, the requirements and application for this certification will be available online at *www.amhca.org/career/credential*.

	*Phase 4a board certification:* AMHCA Clinical Mental Health Counseling Specialist (CMHC Specialist), board-certified in one or more specialization areas

Candidates should consult *AMHCA Standards for the Practice of Clinical Mental Health Counseling*, which lists the applicable knowledge and skills for the specialization they are applying for. *AMHCA Standards* is included in "Essentials" as Appendix B and can be downloaded free at *www.amhca.org/publications/standards*.
Requirements:
Be a Clinical Member of AMHCA.
Have completed all of the licensing requirements as defined by the respective state and have been awarded the license to practice independently. As an independent practitioner, the applicant must have practiced independently for a minimum of three years after completing all state licensure requirements.
Demonstrated clinical mental health counseling expertise in one or more specialties: 　❏　Specialist in Child and Adolescent Counseling 　❏　Specialist in Couples and Family Counseling 　❏　Specialist in Developmental and Learning Disabilities Counseling 　❏　Specialist in Forensic Evaluation 　❏　Specialist in Geriatric Counseling

- ❑ Specialist in Integrated Behavioral Health Care Counseling
- ❑ Specialist in Military Counseling
- ❑ Specialist in Substance Use Disorders and Co-occurring Disorders
- ❑ Specialist in Trauma Counseling

To be recognized as an AMHCA Clinical Mental Health Counseling Specialist, board-certified in one or more specialization areas, the applicant must complete **all** of the following requirements for **each area of specialization** (A, B, C, D):

A. Complete professional development in each specialist area by at least 90 hours of professional development specifically related to the specialist area. These 90 hours must be documented by the date, course title, and number of course hours. Please note the following criteria:

1. One completed post-master's degree graduate semester credit hour is equal to 15 professional development hours.
2. Presentation hours specifically and primarily related to the specialist area can be counted for up to 60 hours of the required professional development hours.
3. Post-graduate courses taught by the applicant specifically and primarily related to the specialist area can be counted for up to 60 hours (a graduate semester hour taught equals 15 contact hours).
4. At least 15 of the 90 professional development hours must be earned within the past five years.
5. Only professional development hours completed within the past 15 years will be counted toward meeting the specialist training requirement.
6. All professional development hours must be completed post-master's degree in Mental Health Counseling or a related counseling field.
7. Hours used for one specialist area cannot be applied to an additional specialist area application.
8. Alternatively, AMHCA members who are fully licensed for independent practice for five years in an area directly related to the specialty applied can document this license in lieu of documenting professional development hours in the specialty area (e.g., an LCMHC who is also fully licensed for five years as an LMFT can be awarded certification as a Specialist in Couples and Family Counseling).

B. Applicants must complete at least 100 hours of face-to-face counseling in the specialist area.

C. Applicants must attest to having completed a minimum of 10 hours of specialist supervision by a licensed mental health professional who has expertise in the area. Supervision required for independent state licensure cannot be counted toward this specialist supervision requirement.

D. Applicants must attest that they have the knowledge of the ethics and standards of practice in the specialist area and will abide by all applicable codes of ethics.

E. Complete the online application and pay the application processing fee to become an AMHCA Clinical Mental Health Counseling Specialist, board-certified in one or more specialization areas (CMHC Specialist).

Successful applicants will be awarded a certificate and will be allowed to display the corresponding digital badge. They may refer to themselves as an "AMHCA Clinical Mental Health Counseling Specialist" or "CMHC Specialist" (e.g., CMHC Specialist–Trauma). For more information, go to *www.amhca.org/career/credential/apply*.

	*Phase 4b board certification:* AMHCA Clinical Mental Health Counseling Diplomate (CMHC Diplomate), board-certified in advanced clinical mental health counseling practice

Requirements:
Be a Clinical Member of AMHCA. Individuals applying to become a CMHC Diplomate spend 50 percent or more of their professional hours in clinical practice.
Have completed all of the licensing requirements as defined by the respective state and have been awarded the license to practice independently. As an independent practitioner, the applicant must have practiced independently for a minimum of five years after completing all state licensure requirements.

Demonstrated advanced practice in clinical mental health counseling beyond the level of independent practice licensing, with verifiable competence (e.g., ongoing participation in private or group clinical practice; leadership roles in state or national mental health organizations; past awards or acknowledgments as a Clinical Mental Health Counselor; regular participation in continuing education activities; etc.).
 	
Advanced General Practice Criteria require that the applicant meet **all of the following requirements** (A, B, C, D, E):
 	
A. Document professional organization service beyond general membership for at least two years (e.g., serving on a licensing board, on a state chapter board, in an executive or committee position for a professional clinical organization, etc.).
 	
B. Attest to having completed 120 hours of continuing education in clinical mental health counseling during the last four consecutive years. If submitting, at the same time, for the CMHC Specialist, only 60 of the 120 hours may be counted simultaneously for both credentialing certifications. Continuing education that applicants have attested to may be audited by AMHCA.
 	
C. Certify that you have read and will abide by *The Clinical Mental Health Counselor Declaration, AMHCA Standards for the Practice of Clinical Mental Health Counseling,* and *AMHCA Code of Ethics,*
 	
D. List the events and dates where you have demonstrated ongoing participation in mental health related activities beyond clinical practice (e.g., lectures, panels, workshops, webinars; community mental health activities; awards received, etc.).
 	
E. Additional experience that includes **two** of the following:
  1. Three years of additional practice at the highest level of clinical licensing available in the applicant's state for a total of eight years fully licensed at the highest level – or –
  2. Three years of graduate teaching in clinical mental health counseling (full-time or part-time) – or –
  3. Three years of experience as a clinical supervisor – or –
  4. Additional credential (e.g., completed requirements as an Approved AAMFT Supervisor, CCMHC, ACS, LADAC, CAP, etc.) – or –
  5. A doctorate in Counselor Education or a doctorate related to the profession of clinical mental health counseling – or –
  6. Publishing a book or making another contribution that adds to the advancement of mental health for the public or the advancement of the profession.

Chapter 3: Career Guidance and the Phases of Professional Development for LCMHCs

F. Complete the online application and pay the application processing fee to become a CMHC Diplomate, board-certified in advanced clinical mental health counseling practice.

Successful applicants will be awarded a certificate and will be allowed to display the corresponding digital badge. They may refer to themselves as an "AMHCA Clinical Mental Health Counseling Diplomate" or "CMHC Diplomate." For more information, go to *www.amhca.org/career/credential/apply/diplomate.*

Phase 4c board certification:

AMHCA Clinical Mental Health Counseling Fellow (CMHC Fellow), board-certified in clinical mental health counseling education and research

Requirements:

Be a Clinical Member of AMHCA. Individuals applying to become a CMHC Fellow spend 50 percent or more of their professional hours in counseling education and research.

Have completed all of the licensing requirements as defined by the respective state and have been awarded the license to practice independently. The applicant must have been licensed to practice independently for a minimum of five years.

Demonstrated advanced counselor education and/or research in the field of clinical mental health counseling beyond the initial level of teaching or research, with verifiable competence.

Advanced Education and Research Criteria require that the applicant meet **all of the following requirements** (A, B, C, D):

A. Document service to the profession for at least two years (e.g., serving on a licensing board, on a state chapter board, in an executive or committee position for a professional clinical organization, etc.).

B. A doctorate in Counselor Education or a doctorate related to the profession of clinical mental health counseling.

C. Graduate-level instruction and/or research that has had a demonstrated impact beyond the academic institution, which specifically contributes to the profession of clinical mental health counseling, and includes both of the following:

- ❏ Seven years of full-time teaching graduate courses and/or research.
- ❏ Publication of one or more texts, four or more peer-reviewed journal articles, or equivalent evidence of published research.

D. **One** of the following:

1. Three years of experience as a clinical supervisor in an academic or research setting – or –
2. The documented development of an approved new course of study, or the development of an approved new research proposal, or other mental health professional accomplishments in teaching and/or research that specifically contributes to the profession of clinical mental health counseling (e.g., theory-building, public policy, professional practice, social justice, etc.).

> E. Complete the online application and pay the application processing fee to become a CMHC Fellow).
>
> Successful applicants will be awarded a certificate and will be allowed to display the corresponding digital badge. They may refer to themselves as an "AMHCA Clinical Mental Health Counseling Fellow," or "CMHC Fellow." For more information, go to *www.amhca.org/career/credential/apply/fellow*.

LCMHCs can apply for multiple Phase 4 AMHCA board certifications. Applicants can also apply for more than one area of specialization as an AMHCA Clinical Mental Health Counseling Specialist. For example, an LCMHC could apply to become a CMHC Specialist in Military Counseling as well as a CMHC Specialist in Substance Use and Co-occurring Disorders. This same LCMHC could also apply to become a CMHC Diplomate or a CMHC Fellow.

Phase 5—LCMHC Recognized for Exceptional Service to the Profession

The AMHCA CMHC Laureate board certification (CMHC Laureate) recognizes exceptional service to the profession. The CMHC Laureate is obtained through peer-nomination and approved by the AMHCA board of directors. The award is based on major contributions to the profession of clinical mental health counseling.

Phase 5 board certification:
AMHCA Clinical Mental Health Counseling Laureate (CMHC Laureate), board-certified for exceptional service to the profession
Requirements:
Have completed all of the licensing requirements as defined by the respective state and have been awarded the license to practice independently. The applicant must have been licensed to practice independently for a minimum of 10 years.
This is an award of excellence that is approved by the AMHCA board of directors.
The CMHC Laureate is a nominated award that is based on major contributions to the profession of clinical mental health counseling.
Nominations will include all of the following:
A. Nominees for this award will typically have earned at least one of the following AMHCA Advanced Professional Board Certifications:

Chapter 3: Career Guidance and the Phases of Professional Development for LCMHCs

> - ❏ Diplomate and Clinical Mental Health Specialist
> - ❏ AMHCA Clinical Mental Health Counseling Specialist, board-certified in one or more specialization areas
> - ❏ AMHCA Clinical Mental Health Counseling Diplomate, board-certified in advanced clinical mental health counseling practice
> - ❏ AMHCA Clinical Mental Health Counseling Fellow, board-certified in clinical mental health counseling education and research
>
> B. The nomination will be a one-page document that lists the specific contributions that the nominee has made to the profession. Individuals may self-nominate.
>
> C. In addition to the one-page nominating document, the nomination will be attested to by at least three letters of endorsement by AMHCA members.
>
> D. The award of the CMHC Laureate will be approved by a selection committee made of three or more members of AMHCA's board of directors.
>
> Successful applicants will be awarded a certificate and will be allowed to display the corresponding digital badge. They may refer to themselves as "AMHCA Clinical Mental Health Counseling Laureate," or "CMHC Laureate."

Developing a Career in Clinical Mental Health Counseling

It is hoped that AMHCA credentialing certifications will inspire all members of the profession to continuously achieve higher levels of professional development. AMHCA members are encouraged to consider how the credentialing certifications will benefit them and those they serve professionally.

Other Career Guidance Considerations

State Laws and Rules

The profession of clinical mental health counseling is governed in each state and the District of Columbia by both laws and rules. Laws are passed by the state legislatures or other legislative bodies. State laws typically authorize the establishment of the profession and stipulate the basic requirements for the profession. State laws also assign certain government agencies to oversee the implementation of the laws and regulate the profession.

These government agencies typically regulate a number of professions through state employees and a licensing board. These agencies enact rules that implement state laws and enforce compliance with governing regulations for each profession. They handle administrative functions, such as reviewing and approving or disapproving applications for licensure. They also may have an investigative staff to examine LCMHCs or other professionals who may not be in compliance with the laws, rules or the codes of ethics of their state. Many other functions may be assigned to these government agencies.

LCMHCs must be aware of the laws and rules as well as the codes of ethics that govern their profession. They are subject to inspection and possible disciplinary action if they do not comply with the laws or rules of their jurisdiction. Laws and rules are generally enacted to protect members of the public from injurious actions or unethical practice by licensed professionals (not to protect the interests of the members of the profession). As noted below, it is important for LCMHCs to be covered by liability insurance.

Liability Insurance:

Regardless of career level, CMHC Students who are in their practicum or internship, Supervised CMHCs, and LCMHCs, should consider obtaining liability insurance. It is recommended that Student CMHC interns provide a copy of a certificate of insurance to their supervisors. Supervised CMHCs should have a copy on file with their agency.

Agencies who employ CMHC Students, Supervised CMHCs, and LCMHCs may provide some liability insurance coverage. However, individually procured liability insurance often offers more complete coverage for individuals than the agency insurance may provide. For more information about liability insurance, consider consulting with AMHCA's insurance partner, CPH & Associates, *www.cphins.com*.

Trauma-Informed Care

Nearly everyone who is in practice will encounter individuals with Post-Traumatic Stress Disorder (PTSD) or other unresolved traumatic or disturbing experiences. Even individuals who present with depression or anxiety or other *DSM–5* disorders often have suffered chronic distress or trauma. For example, individuals who are diagnosed with Borderline Personality Disorder have rates of traumatic experience in excess of 90 percent. It is crucial for all members of the profession to be knowledgeable about trauma-informed care.

Trauma-informed care requires LCMHCs, Supervised CMHCs, and CMHC Students to be well-versed in understanding trauma and anxiety symptomatology. In addition, they must be able to understand the underlying causes of PTSD and other distressing anxiety conditions. Clinicians have access to a number of mental health assessments that assist in developing case conceptualization.

Here are a few examples:

- Adverse Childhood Experiences (ACE) Questionnaire
- Adverse Childhood Experiences International Questionnaire (ACE-IQ)
- *DSM-5* Self-Rated Level 1 Cross-Cutting Symptom Measure—Adult
- World Health Organization Assessment Schedule 2.0 (WHODAS 2.0)

The *AMHCA Standards for the Practice of Clinical Mental Health Counseling* in Appendix B includes a section on Trauma-Informed Care and includes applicable knowledge and skills. LCMHCs who are not qualified to provide evidenced-based treatment for trauma and chronic distress should have a list of reliable specialists for referrals. AMHCA offers credentialing certification as an AMHCA Clinical Mental Health Counseling Specialist in Trauma. (See the qualifications required for *Phase 4a board certification: AMHCA Clinical Mental Health Counseling Specialist, board-certified in one or more specialization areas,* earlier in this chapter).

Integrated Behavioral Health Care

There is a growing degree of overlap between medical treatment and behavioral health. Increasingly, primary care physicians recognize the importance of referring to LCMHCs or other behavioral health specialists for trauma, depression, anxiety, substance use, and other disorders. Therefore, it is incumbent for LCMHCs to recognize physical health concerns and refer individuals to seek medical resources.

LCMHCs are encouraged to consult the section on Integrated Behavioral Health Care in the *AMHCA Standards for the Practice of Clinical Mental Health Counseling* in Appendix B. It includes a section on Integrated Behavioral Health and the applicable knowledge and skills. LCMHCs who work with medical professionals should consider becoming an AMHCA Clinical Mental Health Counseling Specialist in Integrated Behavioral Health Care Counseling, as outlined in *Phase 4a board certification: AMHCA Clinical Mental Health Counseling Specialist, board-certified in one or more specialization areas,* earlier in this chapter.

Chapter 3: Career Guidance and the Phases of Professional Development for LCMHCs

Substance Use Disorders and Co-occurring Disorders

There is a growing need for all LCMHCs to be trained in Substance Use Disorder (SUD) symptomatology, assessment, and evidence-based treatment. Many families experience one or more family members with addition. There are virtually no exceptions to the fact that an individual with an SUD will also be suffering from one or more other *DSM–5* disorders. In many cases, there is a history of chronic anxiety or trauma. Treatment for SUDs requires an understanding of evidence-based approaches that successfully address all of the disorders.

LCMHCs are commonly trained to recognize and treat SUDs and co-occurring disorders. Because of the complexity of these conditions, those LCMHCs who work in this area are highly encouraged to obtain postgraduate training. AMHCA also offers credentialing certification as an AMHCA Clinical Mental Health Counseling Specialist in Substance Use Disorders and Co-occurring Disorders, which is outlined in *Phase 4a board certification: AMHCA Clinical Mental Health Counseling Specialist, board-certified in one or more specialization areas,* earlier in this chapter.

Eating Disorders, Gambling, Internet Addiction, Gaming, and Other Behavioral Compulsions

Mental health providers are seeing more cases of individuals who have some form of a behavioral compulsion. Similar to Substance Use Disorders, these disorders are also commonly accompanied by other co-occurring *DSM–5* disorders.

It should be emphasized that these disorders require specialized training and experience. For example, eating disorders are distinctive from SUDs and the other disorders that are discussed in this section. Evidence-based treatment for eating disorders is distinctive. LCMHCs should not assume that their knowledge and skills in one area of expertise can be directly applied to any of these behavioral compulsions. However, each LCMHCs should have a working familiarity with each type of compulsion and be prepared to consult and refer if appropriate.

Supervision

Many LCMHCs may have the opportunity to become supervisors at some point in their careers. State requirements to be a supervisor vary. Those LCMHCs wishing to supervise other mental health professionals must be aware of and compliant with all requirements that are covered in state laws and rules. There are a number of state or nationally sanctioned training programs. LCMHCs who wish to become supervisors should review all the laws and rules associated with supervisor requirements and obtain both initial qualifying training as well as continuing education.

Counselor Education

The clinical mental health counseling profession depends on the education of new Clinical Mental Health Counseling Students (CMHC Students). Experienced LCMHCs may want to consider employment as part-time or full-time instructors. Individuals who obtain doctoral degrees in counselor education or related courses of study are referred to in the profession as "counselor educators." Many counselor educator programs are accredited by the Council for Accreditation of Counseling and Related Educational Programs (CACREP).

LCMHCs who want to become qualified as counselor educators should investigate a number of programs. Although it is possible to teach in some graduate clinical mental health counseling programs with just a master's degree, most university programs now require their full-time faculty positions to be filled by individuals with doctoral degrees. Many prefer to employ individuals who have graduated from accredited counselor education degree programs.

For more information about teaching in clinical mental health counseling, consider consulting with a counselor educator who is a member of the Association for Counselor Education and Supervision (ACES). ACES members are familiar with the standards and accreditation of counseling programs. These counselor educators can offer recommendations for those who are exploring this crucial aspect of the profession.

CHAPTER 4

History of the Clinical Mental Health Counseling Profession

Milestones in the Development of the Profession

"Aspiring is the first step in creation."
Anonymous

How has the profession of clinical mental health counseling evolved?

Since 1976, the evolution of clinical mental health counseling has been intertwined with the history of the American Mental Health Counselors Association (AMHCA). This history is relevant because it provides perspective for future generations of Licensed Clinical Mental Health Counselors (LCMHCs). As noted, the term LCMHC is used in the body of this book to also refer to CMHC Students and Supervised CMHCs, who are seeking full licensure.

Recounting some of the profession's milestones showcases the contributions of many members of the profession who impacted the health and well-being of individuals, families, communities, and our nation. LCMHCs today are reaping the benefits of those who have labored over the past 40-plus years to bring a greater measure of health to countless people.

The Origins of the Profession

Clinical mental health counseling is a specialization within the broader profession of counseling. Much like the social work profession, the counseling profession traces its roots to the aftereffects of the Industrial Revolution (1760–1840). This era was associated with advancements in technology, improvements in medicine, greater access to material resources, increased workload productivity, and longer life spans on one hand, but with new social problems and challenges on the other. Among these concerns were:

- The need for a more specialized workforce, which required education and vocational training
- The urbanization of communities
- Increased awareness of child abuse and neglect, poverty, homelessness, crime, pollution, and domestic violence
- Clashes in social norms as diverse cultural groups settled into urban areas
- Gaps in socioeconomic status

Against this historical backdrop, Frank Parsons founded the Boston Vocational Bureau in 1908, which was tasked with helping Boston's citizens match themselves to careers that best fit their unique personalities, interests, abilities, and values. In its first four months of operation, the Boston Vocational Bureau served 80 men and women. That same year, Parsons wrote "Choosing a Vocation," the first book outlining the precursor to the professional counseling process (termed "guidance"), which was published after his death in 1909.

Though he did not live to see it, Parsons' introduction of the guidance process sparked a movement that spread rapidly, earning him the title "the Father of Guidance." In 1909, there were 117 counselors in Boston, and by 1910 there were counselors in 35 cities across the United States. By 1911, the first guidance course was introduced at Harvard University, and by 1913 the first counseling association, the National Vocational Guidance Association (NVGA), was founded. The NVGA provided the counseling profession with its first code of ethics and professional peer-reviewed academic journal. During World War I (1914–1918), counselors aided the U.S. military by administering the Army Alpha and Beta tests, precursors to intelligence tests that assisted the military in identifying appropriate candidates for officer training. Indeed, the guidance movement gained traction in the social sciences by utilizing the scientific method and emphasizing psychometrics, the field of study concerned with theory and technique of psychological measurement.

The first use in professional literature of the term "counselor" to describe professionals who implemented the guidance process was in "Workbook in Vocations," written in 1931 by William Martin Proctor, Charles

Gilbert Wrenn, and Glidden Ross Benefield. During the 1930s, some notable counselors proposed that the counseling profession should expand beyond its focus on vocation and career to the prevention and treatment of mental disorders. For example, John M. Brewer, in his book "Education as Guidance" (1932), proposed that counselors could prevent or ameliorate mental illness by providing guidance on mental hygiene—including relationships, citizenship, leisure and recreation, personal well-being, ethics, civil cooperation, and wholesome and cultural action (including the advancement of civil rights for racial minorities).

In 1939, E.G. Williamson published his book "How to Counsel Students: A Manual of Techniques for Clinical Counselors," coining the term "clinical counselor" to describe counselors who diagnosed and treated disorders, utilized the scientific method, administered and interpreted psychological tests, provided advice to clients, attended to forms of non-verbal communication in session, and recognized the importance of individualized, holistic care. Because of these landmark publications, some scholars in counselor education view the 1930s as the true origin of the clinical mental health counseling specialty.

In 1952, the NVGA and three other counseling organizations (the National Association of Guidance and Counselor Trainers, the Student Personnel Association for Teacher Education, and the American College Personnel Association) merged in an attempt to build a stronger professional voice, forming the American Personnel and Guidance Association (APGA). In 1963, President John F. Kennedy signed the Community Mental Health Act into law. This legislation provided funding for outpatient centers to aid in the process of deinstitutionalization—the process of transitioning patients with severe and persistent mental illness from psychiatric hospitals into the community. These centers were often staffed with professional counselors, which furthered the process of professional counselors shifting focus to the specialized concentration of clinical mental health.

Why Start an Association for Mental Health Counselors?

Until 1976, there was no association that represented the growing number of counselors who worked in the mental health field. James Messina and Nancy Spisso, colleagues at the Escambia County Mental Health Center in Pensacola, FL, determined to create an association. In 1976, their efforts resulted in the formation of the American Mental Health Counselors Association (AMHCA). Connie Messina became the first administrative director of the new association. Though AMHCA was originally founded as an independent association, it was intended that it would become a division of APGA.

With the founding of AMHCA, for the first time, an association existed that exclusively represented counselors specializing in the diagnosis and treatment of mental disorders. That same year, 1976, the State of Virginia created the first license for professional counselors, sparking a chain reaction in other states over the next two decades. Licensure signified that a subset of professional counselors had appropriate education, training, and competency to diagnose and treat mental disorders and could therefore be licensed by state governments as health care providers.

The legal application to establish AMHCA as a nonprofit corporation was first filed in Florida. Within the first year, AMHCA's membership had grown to almost 1,500 members. In 1977, AMHCA's board asked its members whether to continue as a freestanding organization or become an APGA division. When voting closed on Dec. 30, 1977, voting members chose to become a division of APGA by the slimmest of majorities—51 percent. A formal application was submitted to APGA, and APGA welcomed AMHCA as a division at its spring 1978 board meeting.

Two years later (1978), AMHCA founded the National Academy of Certified Clinical Mental Health Counselors (NACCMHC), which created and managed the Certified Clinical Mental Health Counselor (CCMHC) credential that was handed off to the National Board for Certified Counselors (NBCC), established in 1982. In 1981, the Council for Accreditation of Counseling & Related Educational Programs (CACREP) was founded. CACREP eventually became the primary accrediting body for counseling degree programs. In 2009, CACREP merged its Community Counseling and Mental Health Counseling degree programs into one unified clinical mental health counseling degree program, further solidifying the clinical mental health counseling specialty area within the counseling profession.

The founders of AMHCA believed that its name ought to signal the creation of a new profession in the counseling field. This professional distinction recognized counselors who were dedicated to helping individuals overcome mental health problems. The selection of the association's name—American Mental Health Counselors Association—promoted the idea that all counselors in mental health settings should be subsumed under the term "mental health." Messina and Spisso coined the term "Mental Health Counselor" to distinguish counselors whose job descriptions focused on clinical work from other types of counselors such as school counselors, vocational rehabilitation counselors, college counselors, personnel counselors, and counselor educators.

Since its inception, AMHCA has concentrated on working for the clinical mental health counseling profession. Since the early 2000s, AMHCA, the American Association of Marriage and Family Therapists, and other associations have worked together to promote legislation that would include authorized Medicare reimbursement for LCMHCs and Licensed Marriage and Family Therapists. Major legislative initiatives have resulted in federal recognition of LCMHCs for hiring by the U.S. Department of Veterans Affairs and the Department of Defense as well as for TRICARE reimbursement.

When AMHCA's founders originated the term "Clinical Mental Health Counselor," they did not fully anticipate the consequences. Using this descriptor meant that the professional training for mental health counselors would need to emerge from colleges of education and so that the profession could take its place in the field of behavioral medicine alongside psychology and clinical social work. The educational degree programs for counselors at the time were not fully developed to support the concept that their graduates would engage in clinical mental health work.

In 1992, APGA changed its name to the American Counseling Association (ACA). As an association, ACA represented all types of counselors (e.g., Vocational Rehabilitation Counselors, College Counselors, School Counselors, etc.) as well as different aspects of counseling (social justice issues, humanistic counseling, counseling education, etc.), and different regions of counseling branches throughout the United States. ACA must of necessity strive to act on behalf of all its numerous divisions. The ACA Governing Council is comprised of more than 30 individuals with voting rights to represent all of these various interests. As a division of ACA, AMHCA had one vote to speak for the interests of the clinical mental health counseling profession.

In 1998, two of ACA's divisions, AMHCA and the American School Counselor Association (ASCA), elected to become legally and financially separate from ACA. Independently, both associations became incorporated as autonomous, nonprofit corporations that still formally affiliated with ACA. In 2018, ASCA and ACA independently determined to completely disaffiliate. The following year, AMHCA and ACA also approved a joint agreement to disaffiliate because of differing aspirations. However, AMHCA continues to coordinate with ACA and ASCA on issues of mutual interest.

Evolution of Education Programs Related to the Profession

Education and continuing education serve as the foundation of all publicly recognized professions. When AMHCA was first organized, its founders did not fully comprehend that they were developing an entirely new profession—clinical mental health counseling. As a result, for some years there was considerable confusion concerning which graduate educational programs were necessary to support the profession.

However, there is now general consensus that master's degree programs will require 60 semester hours. Since LCMHCs diagnose and treat mental disorders, there is also consensus that their education cover mental disorders as defined in the American Psychiatric Association's *"Diagnostic and Statistical Manual of Mental Disorders,"* commonly referred to as the *"DSM."* This manual specifies the diagnostic criteria for all psychological disorders, and it reflects the World Health Organization's *"International Classification of*

Diseases," which physicians and mental health professionals use to assess health concerns. Both of manuals are regularly revised to keep up with the current research as well as evidence-based pract psychology and medicine.

In addition, graduate programs in clinical mental health counseling have advanced to include group counseling, couples and family counseling, human development across the life span, research and assessment, and other topics that related to the effective work of LCMHCs. The result is the maturity of a profession that is holistically oriented on comprehensive behavioral health, including mental and emotional well-being, relationship efficacy, and total wellness. The profession is distinct from all of the other mental health professions by virtue of the breadth and depth of its educational programs at the graduate level.

AMHCA's Foundational Pillars for the Clinical Mental Health Counseling Profession

Since AMHCA's establishment in 1976, the association has grown on the solid footing of the Six Foundational Pillars that AMHCA formulated for the clinical mental health counseling profession:

1. Professional Association
2. Code of Ethics
3. Accreditation and Education Standards
4. National Certification
5. State Licensure
6. Research

Pillar 1: Professional Association

From its inception, AMHCA was organized to promote clinical mental health counseling as a profession and to advance the interests of those engaged in this profession. Throughout its history, AMHCA has developed relationships with other associations to develop public policy, advocate for improved mental health, and further the aspirations and expertise of Clinical Mental Health Counselor education, continuing education, and career advancement. In 1978, AMHCA became affiliated with the American Counseling Association (ACA). AMHCA continues to form professional relationships with mental health professional associations and related mental health organizations. Although AMHCA and ACA jointly agreed to disaffiliate, the two associations continue to be supportive regarding issues of mutual interest.

AMHCA autonomously determines how to best serve the needs of the profession of clinical mental health counseling and its mental health public-policy requirements. As an association, it will continue to create positive and collaborative working relationships in representing the members of the profession.

Pillar 2: Code of Ethics

Dating back to the first years of AMHCA, the original *AMHCA Code of Ethics* was formulated based on the existing code of ethics of the American Personnel and Guidance Association. The AMHCA *Code of Ethics* was developed to address issues specifically pertaining to the practice of clinical mental health counseling, which generates ethical concerns inherently different from other branches of counseling.

Since then, additional ethical considerations that affect clinical mental health counseling have been written and included. AMHCA continues to update the *AMHCA Code of Ethics*. The association has a standing committee related to ethics, and the *AMHCA Code of Ethics* is subject to immediate revisions when appropriate. The unabridged version of the *AMHCA Code of Ethics* is included in "Essentials" as Appendix C and is available at no cost from *www.amhca.org/publications/ethics*.

Pillar 3: Accreditation and Educational Standards

National educational and accreditation standards for graduate programs in clinical mental health counseling have been a concern for AMHCA's leadership from the outset. These issues continue to be crucial to the needs of the profession.

The establishment of accreditation standards for clinical mental health counseling programs has been challenging because of the various stakeholders, which include AMHCA, state counseling licensing boards, counselor educators, and other interested parties. In 1992, AMHCA President Roberta M. Driscoll asked AMHCA co-founder Jim Messina to spearhead the effort to accredit mental health counseling graduate training programs. He suggested a competency-based model called the Orlando Model that resulted in the creation of the National Commission for Mental Health Counseling. In 1995, this commission published a monograph titled "Mental Health Counseling in the 90s" to identify the competencies needed for mental health counseling and counselor education programs.

The initiative to accredit mental health counseling programs was acquired by the Council for Accreditation of Counseling & Related Educational Programs (CACREP) in 2009. CACREP accredits a number of different counseling educational programs. Only one of these accreditation programs specifically recognizes the specific comprehensive clinical mental health counseling master's degree educational standards.

Prior to 2009, the term "Community Counseling" was the commonly accepted term that counselor educators used. This resulted in the development of about 160 programs. Regrettably, because of all of the variability, this weakened the growth and recognition of the clinical mental health counseling profession. This was resolved when CACREP eliminated the Community Counseling Standards in 2009 and replaced them with Clinical Mental Health Counseling Standards. This accreditation standard for the profession has helped advance the educational requisites of the profession. CACREP continues to revise standards as needed.

In a related development, a number of counselor education programs have been concerned about CACREP requirements that require that the core faculty of master's degree programs be doctoral graduates in counselor education. Because of this requirement, many universities have elected not to adopt CACREP accreditation. However, CACREP accreditation in clinical mental health counseling has been recognized by the U.S. Congress as a requirement for both federal employment and independent TRICARE insurance payments. (TRICARE is the health care program of the U.S. Department of Defense.)

A separate education standard has been developed primarily by Psychologists for those seeking licensure or certification as a master's-level provider of counseling and psychological services. The Masters in Psychology and Counseling Accreditation Council (MPCAC) was created in 1995 to accredit terminal master's degrees in psychology. An independent organization, MPCAC has no financial or formal affiliation with other professional or trade associations such as the American Psychological Association. MPCAC accreditation has not been recognized by the U.S. Congress for either employment in federal jobs or reimbursement by TRICARE.

Although AMHCA has not formally endorsed CACREP or MPCAC accreditation, the association does recognize the benefits of federal employment and reimbursement. The association encourages all graduate programs related to clinical mental health counseling to provide accurate information to those interested in their programs.

Unifying the educational standards for accreditation will continue to be an AMHCA objective. All of the other mental health professions are educationally regulated by a single accreditation standard. It would be beneficial if these two accreditation programs would collaborate in creating an integrated graduate educational accreditation standard.

In addition to educational accreditation standards, AMHCA recognized the need for practice standards, which it first published in 1979. *AMHCA Standards for the Practice of Clinical Mental Health Counseling* has been the cornerstone reference for the profession since that time and has been used to justify federal hiring and reimbursement. In addition to practice standards, this document also addresses issues regarding the graduate training of Clinical Mental Health Counselors as well as faculty and supervisor qualifications.

Because the profession continually evolves, *AMHCA Standards* has been revised in 1992, 1993, 2003, 2011, and 2020. It is worthwhile to note that these standards incorporate: Behavioral Medicine, Evidence-Based Practices, Multicultural Competencies, Neuroscience and the Biological Basis for Behavior, Psychopharmacology, Trauma-Informed Care, and other evolving standards.

Today, *AMHCA Standards* is updated on a continuous basis. The AMHCA Advancement for Clinical Practice Committee meets monthly to revise existing standards and to formulate new standards for the members of the profession. Each standard includes the specified knowledge and itemized skills associated with that standard. The unabridged version of the 2020 edition of *AMHCA Standards for the Practice for Clinical Mental Health Counseling* is included in "Essentials" as Appendix B and is available at no cost from *www.amhca.org/publications/standards*.

Pillar 4: National Certification

In 1976, AMHCA's leadership understood that Clinical Mental Health Counselors would have to be licensed. As a precursor to licensure, a national certification was deemed essential in order to establish the credibility of the profession. In 1979, Jim Messina, AMHCA's then president, was instrumental in the creation of the National Academy of Certified Clinical Mental Health Counselors (NACCMHC).

The purpose of the academy was to devise a competency-based assessment model to gain recognition for the first national certification body. The certification model required work samples from candidates and resulted in the award of the Certified Clinical Mental Health Counselor (CCMHC). The National Academy then allied with the National Board for Certified Counselors (NBCC) to request inclusion of the CCMHC as one of a number of advanced certifications open to those individuals who had earned the National Certified Counselor (NCC) credential.

With state licensure for LCMHCs now recognized in all 50 states and the District of Columbia, certification has become more focused on recognizing professional competence and achievement. In recent years, AMHCA has promoted advanced practice certification for seasoned LCMHCs.

Starting in 2012, AMHCA established the Diplomate and Clinical Mental Health Specialist (DCMHS) credential to recognize those LCMHCs who had achieved superior practice qualifications and who had become specialists. Criteria were developed to ascertain 1) advanced practice certification as a Diplomate and 2) qualification for areas of specialized practice. This objective was accomplished so that LCMHCs could provide members of the public as well as interested agencies with an independently confirmed certification regarding their postgraduate training and expertise.

As noted in Chapter 3, in 2019, AMHCA approved the replacement of the DCMHS with three separate, *Phase 4—Advanced AMHCA Board Certification for a Clinical Mental Health Counselor:*

- *Phase 4a board certification:* AMHCA Clinical Mental Health Counseling Specialist (CMHC Specialist), board-certified in one or more specialization areas,
  e.g., Trauma (CMHC Specialist–Trauma)

- *Phase 4b board certification:* AMHCA Clinical Mental Health Counseling Diplomate (CMHC Diplomate), board-certified in advanced clinical mental health counseling practice

- *Phase 4c board certification:* AMHCA Clinical Mental Health Counseling Fellow (CMHC Fellow), board-certified in clinical mental health counseling education and research

All of these board certifications are based on graduate education, licensure, work experience, and advanced training. Additional information about AMHCA's Credentialing and Board Certification program can be found in Chapter 3 of "Essentials" and at *www.amhca.org/career/credential*.

Additionally, AMHCA recognizes LCMHCs who have made extraordinary contributions to the profession:

❑ *Phase 5 board certification:* AMHCA Clinical Mental Health Counseling Laureate (CMHC Laureate), board-certified for exceptional service to the profession

Also in 2019, AMHCA approved the recognition of three initial credentialing phases of career development, with members' eligibility based on meeting corresponding qualifications: For more information on Phases 1–3 credentials—CMHC Student Credential, Supervised CMHC Credential, and Independent CMHC Credential—see Chapter 3.

Pillar 5: State Licensure

In 1978, Virginia became the first state to recognize licensure for mental health counselors. Three years later, legislation was passed in Florida to establish Licensed Mental Health Counselors. These pioneering legislative efforts were instrumental in spurring other states to adopt licensure laws and in establishing regulatory state counseling boards. In 2014, California became the last state to pass licensure for mental health counseling.

As licensure laws were passed, states used different license titles. The most common state license titles are "Professional Counselor" and "Mental Health Counselor." Usually, the term "Licensed" is added to the official title, as in "Licensed Professional Counselor" (LPC) or "Licensed Mental Health Counselor" (LMHC). Regardless of the various state license titles, all mental health counselors who are licensed to assess, diagnose, and treat mental health disorders are designated by AMHCA as Licensed Clinical Mental Health Counselors. This term accurately describes the work that LCMHCs do, no matter what their license title is.

Because the American Counseling Association (ACA) represents all types of counselors, it has urged the adoption of "Licensed Professional Counselor" as the license title for all state-licensed counselors, even if other counselors have not been clinically trained to diagnose or treat mental disorders (e.g., Vocational Rehabilitation Counselors, School Counselors, etc.). Because the designation "Licensed Professional Counselor" can describe many different types of counselors, it is ambiguous and it is frequently misunderstood by other mental health professionals and the public. AMHCA prefers the term Licensed Clinical Mental Health Counselor (LCMHC), since the vast majority of state-licensed counselors are legally authorized to diagnose and treat mental disorders by virtue of their education and licensure.

AMHCA's leadership has maintained that whatever the title of the license, those trained and educated in clinical mental health counseling are members of a unique profession. Regardless of license title, they all have the right to be distinguished as a "Licensed Clinical Mental Health Counselor." Increasingly, members of the profession simply identify themselves with this professional title. People readily understand that this designates what they do without the need for further explanation. To avoid misunderstanding, AMHCA designates "Licensed Clinical Mental Health Counselor" (LCMHC) for clinicians and "clinical mental health counseling" for the profession.

Pillar 6: Research

The need for research specific to clinical mental health counseling was acknowledged shortly after AMHCA was established. The *Journal of Mental Health Counseling* was established in 1976 with Bill Weikel as its first editor. The first edition of the *Journal* appeared in 1978 and has been published regularly since then.

The practice of clinical mental health counseling draws on recognized models of psychology and counseling. Consequently, no single theoretical model of counseling has been determined to be objectively superior. However, state licensure laws and regulations formulate a profession that is distinct from psychology, clinical social work, and marriage and family therapy. Although the education of LCMHCs integrates applications from these other professions, clinical mental health counseling incorporates a strengths-based approach that is holistic and correlated with integrated behavioral health and medicine. (See Chapter 1 for more about what makes clinical mental health counseling distinct from the other mental health professions.)

In addition, though research exists on the effectiveness of specific treatment approaches to treat mental disorders (such as Cognitive Behavioral Therapy and psychopharmacology), no specialized body of research exists that documents the specific effectiveness of LCMHCs, or their effectiveness compared with the other mental health professions. This absence of research is presumed to be part of the reason for the general public's lack of awareness of the clinical mental health counseling profession's more clinically focused education and training. Research on the clinical mental health counseling profession warrants greater attention by researchers.

The Impact of Clinical Mental Health Counseling

LCMHCs now make up over one fifth (more than 120,000) of the 502,00 available psychotherapists who are licensed in the United States. The role of LCMHCs as Primary Mental Health Care Providers will continue to increase, because these mental health professionals are remarkably well prepared to address a broad range of mental disorders and other public mental health-related concerns.

Certainly, there is a growing recognition of the necessity of integrating psychological and medical services. See, for example, the robust section of the website of the federal government's Substance Abuse and Mental Health Services Administration (SAMHSA) on integrated care at *www.integration.samhsa.gov/integrated-care-models*. In medicine, psychiatrists alone cannot meet the dramatically swelling demands for psychotherapy. The number of recognized Mental Health Care Health Professional Shortage Areas in the United States is more than 5,000 (see *tinyurl.com/y9u2g69b)*. Mental and emotional well-being is increasingly recognized as a crucial aspect of total health. Research has demonstrated that LCMHCs are becoming ever more decisive in efforts to reduce health care costs and, at the same time, improving health care outcomes.

As the profession of clinical mental health counseling is acknowledged as a key component of comprehensive health initiatives, LCMHCs will gain greater prominence as highly effective Primary Mental Health Care Providers.

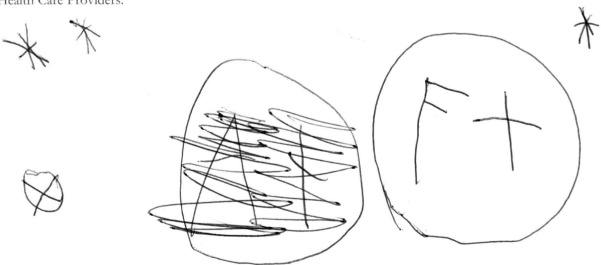

CHAPTER 5

The Future of the Profession

Prospects for Professional Development and
the Development of the Profession

*"It does not matter how slowly you go
as long as you do not stop."*
Confucius

What do we anticipate about the future of the profession?

Because of the education and training that Licensed Clinical Mental Health Counselors (LCMHCs) receive, they are well positioned to provide a breadth of services. This uniquely sets them apart from Social Workers, Marriage and Family Therapists, and Psychologists. Further, LCMHCs are primed and ready to be part of the biggest wave of the future—integrated health care. As noted, the acronym LCMHC is used in the body of this book to also refer to CMHC Students and Supervised CMHCs, who are seeking full licensure.

In expanding their role as Primary Mental Health Care Providers, LCMHCs will continue to have the support of their professional association—the American Mental Health Counselors Association (AMHCA). Since 1976, AMHCA has been dedicated to the advancement of the clinical mental health counseling profession.

AMHCA also advocates for improved behavioral health for every person. The association has partnered with several mental health related associations to urge better, more comprehensive health care and greater access to mental health care services. The future of the profession, however, ultimately rests on the expertise of LCMHCs and their successful treatment of diagnosable mental disorders.

Primary Mental Health Care Providers

Almost everyone from time to time will rely on the medical skill of physicians who are primary care providers. When conditions warrant, primary care providers refer patients to medical specialists, such as cardiologists and surgeons. Regarding the evolution of the mental health professions, there has likewise been a trend toward greater specialization.

For example, in recent decades, Psychologists have focused more on testing, the treatment of psychosis, and other acutely morbid mental disorders. The percentage of Psychiatrists or Psychologists offering psychotherapy has largely diminished. Licensed Clinical Social Workers (LCSWs) continue to provide psychotherapy in a wide variety of circumstances, but a substantial portion of their education and continuing education is devoted to community resources and social justice. Licensed Marriage and Family Therapists (LMFTs) are largely trained in the application of multigenerational family systems theory.

LCMHCs offer evidence-based psychotherapy services. They are rigorously educated and trained as Primary Mental Health Care Providers who are highly skilled in mental health diagnosis and treatment. However, their professional focus extends to an all-inclusive vision of total psychological and physiological health. Additionally, they place substantial emphasis on the capacity of the mind and brain to achieve a greater degree of inherent well-being.

Like a doctor who sets a fracture knowing that the bone will mend and become stronger, LCMHCs resolve mental disorders while also working to develop enhanced mental and emotional resilience. This paradigm of holistic treatment is based on individual strengths. All LCMHCs have this focus on comprehensive well-being, integrated with relationship efficacy and total health and wellness.

In addition, just as most physicians become highly trained in one or more specializations, LCMHCs increasingly are becoming specialists in a variety of mental health care areas. Through independent board certification, AMHCA has recognized those who have sought advanced training and expertise in specialist areas (see Chapter 3). As noted earlier, these specializations include trauma resolution, substance use and co-occurring disorders, child and adolescent pediatric mental health concerns, developmental and learning disabilities, the special needs of military individuals and their families, and couples and family mental health.

Approaching Advancements of the Clinical Mental Health Counseling Profession

Because of the distinctive education, licensing, and professional emphasis of LCMHCs, they will continue to play a prominent role in the advancement of comprehensive health practice and research. Of great interest is the growing demand for integrated behavioral mental health care as part of overall health care. A growing number of physicians and health care facilities—such as clinics, hospitals, and other medical institutions—recognize the absolute imperative of incorporating mental health services into medical treatment protocols.

As an example, while physicians diagnose and medically treat diabetes, LCMHCs can provide the continuity of care that is essential for successful treatment outcomes through their work with diabetes patients. This includes prescription compliance and the adoption of diet, exercise, and lifestyle changes. LCMHCs can also address underlying mental and emotional concerns that are crucial in treating chronic medical conditions such as diabetes, gastrointestinal disorders, and injury-related disabilities. To illustrate this further, many individuals who habitually admit themselves to emergency rooms have unmet mental health concerns. By referring these individuals to LCMHCs who have postgraduate training in integrated behavioral health care, the instance of emergency room visits is decreased.

These examples highlight some of the ways in which LCMHCs are Primary Mental Health Care Providers. AMHCA anticipates that LCMHCs will substantially contribute to reduced overall health costs while simultaneously playing a major role in achieving higher rates of successful outcomes.

Public Health Issues of the Clinical Mental Health Counseling Profession

Many community problems—including those related to bullying, poverty, violence, discrimination, and criminal justice issues—have a mental health component. AMHCA recognizes that many societal problems not only affect individuals' lives and relationships, but result in economic and mental health burdens on individuals, families, and communities.

Everyone knows, works with, or is related to someone who experiences needless suffering. In their work, LCMHCs witness the toll that distress, disorders, and disease take on individuals, couples, and families. These health burdens also affect the communities we live in; in fact, they result in public health impairments of major import.

Integrated care is one way that health professionals across the United States are working to improve the nation's health. Integrated care recognizes that poor physical health affects mental health, and vice versa. For example, diabetes is treated medically, but responds well to integrated care because medical care cannot be effective if the person being treated does not comply with the doctor's instructions for diet, prescription medication, and physical activity—all of which affect quality of life and mental health.

A growing number of LCMHCs work in integrated care settings to help bridge treatment for physical conditions (such as diabetes, cardiac problems, cancer, and physical trauma) with the mental health effects that may result (such as anxiety, depression, substance use, and mental trauma). Integrating mental health, substance use, and primary care services produces the best outcomes and is the nation's best chance for improving the nation's public health. AMHCA continuously advocates for public policy that proactively addresses public health concerns. It is imperative that professional organizations, public interest groups, and legislative bodies create practical, cost-effective solutions to these problems. A failure to deal with them societally or legislatively now—even if the solution costs money in the near-term—will produce unreasonably expensive outcomes for individuals and families in the long-term.

Following is an outline of many of these public health concerns:

- ❑ Health Care Related Mental Health Concerns
  - o Health Care
  - o Family Issues
  - o Violent Behavior
  - o Education
- ❑ Economic-Related Mental Health Concerns
  - o Economic Inequality
  - o Employee Workplace Issues
- ❑ National and Community-Related Mental Health Concerns
  - o Public Fairness
  - o Climate Change
  - o Gun Control
  - o Immigration
  - o Criminal Justice and Prison Health Care

Health Care Related Mental Health Concerns

Health Care

- ❑ *Uninsured individuals and families:* The lack of health care coverage, including access to mental health services, continues to plague children, adults, families, and communities. Many individuals and policymakers still do not realize how much prevention, routine access to services, and adequate care would reduce disease and improve health while also decreasing medical costs.

- ❑ *High costs of care, medications, etc.:* The growing costs of medical services and prescription medications result in unnecessary mental and medical health conditions.

- ❑ *Elder care:* In particular, our nation's failure to provide comprehensive integrated health services for the elderly affects individuals who no longer have the resources to care for themselves.

- ❑ *Uneven quality of care:* As a nation, we are fortunate that many individuals do have access to health insurance. Even so, the disparity of care is appalling. Often the care depends on insurance decisions that do not consider the actual impact beyond economic costs.

- ❑ *Lack of assess to co-morbid treatment for substance use addiction, and ineffective treatment for behavioral compulsions:* Another concern is that many suffer from substance use and behavioral compulsive disorders such as self-harm and eating disorders. These conditions are strongly correlated with other mental health disorders such as trauma, generalized anxiety, and depression. Without comprehensive care for the root causes of these comorbid conditions, the suffering of patients and their families will continue indefinitely. By contrast, integrated behavioral health care combined with mental health care produces lasting, positive outcomes. Health costs decline and former patients develop more satisfying and productive lives. For example, The American Disabilities Act has enabled many individuals to make meaningful contributions to society while enjoying greater health and well-being.

- ❑ *Stigma associated with mental health care that deters those who need it from seeking it:* Fortunately, the stigma associated with seeking mental health has been significantly reduced. Many individuals no longer fear being judged if they seek help from an LCMHC or other mental health professional.

Regrettably, some individuals still will not seek out psychotherapy or counseling because they believe only weak or incapable people need to see a "shrink." Some also worry that seeing a mental health professional will adversely affect their employment, their relationships, or other aspects of their lives. Hopefully, more people will realize that just as people occasionally need the skilled services of a doctor, they may benefit from seeing a mental health professional.

- *Shortage of licensed mental health professionals in rural areas:* Fewer and fewer medical and mental health professionals work in rural areas with low population density. People who live outside urban areas may not have access to a licensed mental health professional. Some have to travel many miles to find a qualified therapist or counselor, or the travel is such a deterrent that they forgo mental health services altogether. The emergence of tele-mental health services has offered one possible solution. Also, some LCMHCs and others make weekly trips to multiple towns in rural areas. Whatever the solution, everyone should have access to competent medical mental health care.

- *Seniors' lack of access to professional mental health services because of current Medicare restrictions:* Few people are aware that seniors who are covered by Medicare do not have access to Licensed Clinical Mental Health Counselors and Licensed Marriage and Family Therapists. When Medicare legislation was written in the 1970s, only Licensed Psychologists and Licensed Clinical Social Workers were authorized to receive Medicare reimbursement for services. This oversight can only be corrected through congressional legislation. Without passage of Medicare reimbursement, seniors will continue to have restricted access to qualified mental health care services.

- *Shortage of licensed mental health professionals in treating co-occurring medical and mental health disorders:* Individuals seeking treatment for mental health concerns are often diagnosed with two or more disorders. For example, those who have a substance addiction may also have depression, anxiety, PTSD, or some other comorbid condition. Virtually all LCMHCs receive graduate education in treating co-occurring disorders, as well as training in dealing with addictions and compulsive behaviors. In addition, they receive education in integrated behavioral health. Without comprehensive treatment approaches, individuals with multiple disorders will receive inadequate treatment with poor outcomes.

Family Issues

- *Child care:* Progress has been made in providing options for child care. Still, much remains to be done to ensure that all children are competently cared for and that their parents can provide sufficient income well above the poverty line.

- *Youth and developmental trauma:* Increasingly, mental health professionals treat children and adolescents for developmental trauma. These conditions arise from multiple sources that, if left untreated, create continuing problems throughout childhood and into adulthood. More mental health professionals need additional education to effectively treat these conditions.

- *Paid family leave:* The first weeks and months of an infant's life are crucial to psychological and physiological development. The need for suitable family leave can affect the well-being of children throughout the life span. Parents and children need these formative months to bond in order to establish the foundation for secure family relationships.

Violent Behavior

- *Domestic violence, including intimate partner violence and child abuse:* Unfortunately, the effects of domestic violence—including intimate partner violence and child abuse—have a negative impact on families and communities, and generate continuing adverse consequences if not addressed. Men and women offenders who have received effective treatment demonstrate high rates of recovery from their prior behavioral patterns. It's also important to recognize that family members who have been subjected to violence require mental and emotional support. If that support is not made available, they will face enduring consequences. In contrast, those who have received mental health resources will enjoy greater life satisfaction.

- ❏ *Community violence:* The concept that "it takes a community to raise a child" has received renewed interest. Violence can only be addressed when neighbors and family members receive needed support from governmental agencies, including law enforcement. Individuals who commit violence should be dealt with equitably in the justice system. When appropriate, they should be referred to mental health care providers so that they can learn how to positively change their lives.

- ❏ *Oppressive police behaviors:* Many law enforcement agencies now offer increased training to understand mental health conditions and to deal with offenders in more effective ways. While effective reviews of oppressive police actions are important, so is more community support for law enforcement officers. Community–police dialogues led by LCMHCs and other mental health professionals are just one way to foster better understanding and cooperation.

- ❏ *Elder-care abuse:* Elder-care abuse is highly destructive, and the potential for its occurrence increases when families do not have the resources to support older family members. The challenges of caring for the elderly include providing mental health care for them as well as for the family members or others responsible for ensuring their safety and wellness.

- ❏ *Sexual abuse and harassment:* Sexual abuse and harassment in the workplace must be effectively addressed. Better human resources training in recognizing and preventing abuse is paramount. More attention to providing support for victims is essential. Conversely, to preclude future incidents of abuse and harassment, offenders need adequate treatment protocols. Another crucial issue that affects the health of communities is human trafficking and the virtual enslavement of children and adults in prostitution, pornography, and other forms of sexual exploitation. Increased public awareness is crucial. Additionally, adequate mental health care services must be provided to those who have been traumatized and victimized.

- ❏ *Bullying and internet harassment and abuse:* Bullying has some similarities with abuse and harassment, and internet harassment is becoming a significant mental health concern. When offenders are identified, they need to be confronted with the consequences of their behaviors and they need to receive efficacious therapy.

Education

The future of our families and our communities relies on effective education. Economic security is dependent on training, skills attainment, and career development. Unique among mental health care providers, LCMHCs receive graduate education in vocational guidance. Often, mental health support for an individual's occupational concerns can reduce anxiety and increase personal satisfaction.

- ❏ *Barriers to higher education:* With rising levels of student loan indebtedness, individuals may face years of economic insecurity. Likewise, those with limited access to education may well experience less workplace productivity and occupational satisfaction and more work insecurity.

- ❏ *Early childhood education concerns:* Educational opportunities should begin in the first years of life. And, resources for training and education ought to be available well into adulthood. Just as news of individuals receiving diplomas in later years is met with cheer and approval, we all need to celebrate and pursue continuing education, regardless of age.

Economic Related Mental Health Concerns

Economic Inequality

- ❏ *Income inequality:* Economists have shown for many years the growing disparity between the wealthiest and those whose income is insufficient to economic security. This inequality continues to shrink the middle class, whose incomes and spending have historically produced the greatest benefits for the national economy.

- ❑ *Gender and racial disparity in compensation and professional advancement:* This income disproportion is also reflected in gender and racial inequalities in earnings. Single parents who are women and people of color face income uncertainties that correlate with chronic anxiety and depression. Support for training, the elimination of advancement discrimination, and access to comprehensive integrated health care services are requirements that will need local, state, and national investments if we are to avoid wasting human potential.

Employee Workplace Issues

- ❑ *Work–family conflict, excessive work hours, and workplace toxin exposures:* In the workplace, many organizations are paying greater attention to solving work-family conflicts, because doing so ensures greater productivity. Employers who abuse their workers create economic costs for their enterprises and for their communities. Excessive work hours; workplace toxin exposures; and inadequately addressing health, safety, and environmental hazards ultimately result in higher costs for everyone.

- ❑ *Economic insecurity, vulnerability, and insufficient income for living expenses:* Insufficient income to meet the necessities of living results in economic insecurity and vulnerability. The physical and mental impact on adults and children cannot be adequately measured. Effective workplace policies of the past (the 40-hour workweek, child labor laws, etc.) have greatly benefited society. As enlightened businesses and other organizations realize human benefits as well as improved profitability, self-regulation will yield greater results. Government regulation and mental health consultation will also play a crucial role in establishing improved economic vitality for many.

National and Community Related Mental Health Concerns

Public Fairness

- ❑ *Racial injustice:* For everyone who is a mental health care provider, offering ethical care must be irrespective of race, national origin, gender identity, sexual orientation, age, and any other factor that might impede treatment.

- ❑ *LGBTQ+ rights:* Just as validly, the mental health professions support the need to correct any inequality related to racial injustice, LGBTQ+ rights, and all other injurious biases. Individuals who are harmfully intolerant or discriminatory deal with personal insecurity and anxiety that can be addressed. Similarly, groups that foster narrow-mindedness can be helped to become more empathetic.

Climate Change

- ❑ *Environmental regulation:* The increasing public awareness of environmental issues, particularly climate change, will promote greater support for positive transformation. Governmental policy is one resource for creating cost-effective, improved, and beneficial regulations.

- ❑ *Major weather effects on communities:* We all have a responsibility to care for our planet. This concept of stewardship applies to each person. Major weather effects on communities will continue to impact public health and individual wellness. Mental health care along with adequate medical resources will be central to dealing with these effects.

Gun Control

- *Background checks:* Another growing concern is the frequency of gun violence and its impact on families, schools, and communities. Sensible measures can be taken to ensure effective background checks. While the rights of individuals need to be heeded, these rights should never override the needs of individuals to be secure and free of fear.

- *Impact of mass shootings on families, schools, and communities:* Mass shootings can be addressed, and people will feel more at ease if local, state, and national governments find realistic, workable solutions.

Immigration

- *Refugee and asylum policy, and migrant camps and detention:* The United States of America has always been a refuge for immigrants. It's imperative that the nation has effective asylum policies in place so that individuals and families can find sanctuary from intolerable conditions. In dealing with increasing numbers of refugees, adequate provisions for humane treatment must continue to be an imperative.

- *Judicial blockages for immigration hearings, and lack of access to legal counsel:* Likewise, immigrants need appropriate and affordable access to legal counsel and timely judicial hearings.

Criminal Justice and Prison Health Care

- *Drug sentencing disparities:* Criminal justice disparities must continue to be addressed. The high number of incarcerated nonviolent offenders in the United States could be treated in alternative ways. This intolerable situation is disproportionately experienced by minority populations in the sentencing for violent crimes as well as for nonviolent offenses.

- *Treatment rather than jail for people with severe mental health conditions:* Rather than automatically imprisoning offenders, greater efforts need to be made to provide reasonable alternatives for treatment, service, in-house custody, and rehabilitation. It is more effective to move from blind punishment to initiatives that support individuals in constructive pursuits so that they become invested in contributing to their communities.

- *Ineffective mental health care services for offenders:* In addition, the underlying cause of criminal behaviors must be dealt with. LCMHCs have the training and experience to successfully treat the co-morbid conditions that lead to crime. Effective mental health treatment for incarcerated individuals as well as for those who are recently released can be a viable comprehensive approach that lessens the incidence of recidivism.

Clinical Mental Health Counseling and Improved Public Health

Addressing the public health issues discussed above directly involves the profession of clinical mental health counseling. LCMHCs have the training—and the professional experience—to play an increasingly vital role as mental health care providers. Working with other mental health professionals, policymakers, government officials, public interest groups, and other organizations, we can meet all of these challenges. The result will be improved overall health for individuals, families, communities, and the country.

Chapter 5: The Future of the Profession

AMHCA's Ongoing Initiatives

AMHCA continually engages in new initiatives that promote the profession and advance the understanding of mental, emotional, and relational well-being. Focusing on neuroscience, integrated health, and emerging issues in wellness, AMHCA works with other associations, health providers, and state and national institutions to further evidence-based practice for members of the clinical mental health counseling profession and those they serve.

Current information on the following initiatives is available at *www.amhca.org*:

- ASCENT (AMHCA Strategic Counselor Engagement and Network Technology) Program
- Counseling People With Cancer
- Clinical Quality Issues in Health Care Reform
- End-of-Life Counseling
- Intimate Partner Violence
- Neuroscience Education and Specialization
- New and Emerging Clinical Issues
- Suicide Prevention
- Treatment Strategies to Address Eating Disorders

These and many other future initiatives will shape the practice of clinical mental health counseling.

Creating the Future of the Profession

"Essentials of the Clinical Mental Health Counseling Profession" describes the many strengths of the occupation that LCMHCs have chosen as their vocation. It also lays out a path for LCMHCs who are members of AMHCA to achieve career development and recognition as they acquire increased levels of expertise. LCMHCs are encouraged to fully understand the five phases of professional development for a career in clinical mental health counseling and the corresponding AMHCA Career Development Credentialing (Phases 1–3) and Board Certification (Phases 4–5). For more information, see Chapter 3.

In addition, members are urged to understand the key documents that undergird their profession: *The Clinical Mental Health Counselor Declaration, AMHCA Standards for the Practice of Clinical Mental Health Counseling,* and *AMHCA Code of Ethics* (see Appendixes) and the association's website, *www.amhca.org*. Finally, to enhance their continuing professional development, all LCMHCs can benefit from the *Journal of Mental Health Counseling; The Advocate Magazine;* and AMHCA training, webinars, and conferences.

The future of the profession of clinical mental health counseling rests on the individual and collective efforts of all LCMHCs. As Primary Mental Health Care Providers, LCMHCs advocate for resilient mental health and enriched overall wellness. They share a common vision of individuals and families living more fulfilling lives. It is this vision that will continue to motivate members of the profession to achieve new discoveries in psychology and neuroscience and to then apply them through innovative treatment approaches. They will continue to focus on increased outcome effectiveness to ease distress and improve health. The coming opportunities for LCMHCs have never been as expansive as they are now.

Section 2

PROFESSIONAL ASSOCIATIONS RELATED TO CLINICAL MENTAL HEALTH COUNSELING

CHAPTER 6

The Organization of the American Mental Health Counselors Association

The Association for the Professional of
Clinical Mental Health Counseling

"Any organization is only human."
Rensis Likert

What does AMHCA do to promote the profession?

From its beginning in 1976, the American Mental Health Counselors Association (AMHCA) was established to support those who were engaged in clinical mental health counseling. This primary function of AMHCA has continued since that time without pause.

AMHCA's leadership and staff have contributed to the advancement of the clinical mental health counseling profession. This has been accomplished through its support of initiatives at the national level such as licensure portability, recognition of the profession by the government, and recognition by other mental health related associations. These continuous efforts enhance the status of Licensed Clinical Mental Health Counselors (LCMHCs) in programs for federal hiring and in ongoing endeavors to achieve reimbursement under Medicare. As noted on page 2, the acronym LCMHC is used in the body of this book to also refer to CMHC Students and Supervised CMHCs, who are seeking full licensure.

In addition, AMHCA's leaders have promoted the development of policies and laws that impact the nation's overall appreciation of mental and emotional well-being. The stigma of mental disorders has been reduced in part because AMHCA has partnered with other associations and interest groups to educate legislators, educators, and members of the public.

Additionally, the need for research specific to clinical mental health counseling was acknowledged shortly after AMHCA was established. The *Journal of Mental Health Counseling* was established to advance research for the profession in 1978 and has been published regularly since then. AMHCA's support of research is also evidenced by continuing education through training programs and conferences.

AMHCA's organization is not widely understood. It is hoped that a fuller awareness of what the association does will lead to greater member support and participation. While there are other associations that represent mental health professionals, since its inception, AMHCA has fully focused on the advancement of the profession of clinical mental health counseling.

Since AMHCA will continue to adapt to the varying needs of the profession, the organization outlined below may change over time. The association prides itself on its stability and its capacity to react flexibly to changing requirements that may necessitate organization modifications.

Organization of AMHCA

Since 1998, AMHCA has been incorporated as an independent, nonprofit corporation. The management of the association is described in AMHCA's bylaws and policies. As an association, it advocates for both its members and the profession.

The overall direction of AMHCA is governed by its board of directors, who are elected by AMHCA members. In addition to the board of directors, AMHCA has a number of standing committees with specific responsibilities (see current list in the infographic on the next page). Finally, the staff of the association is directed by an executive director, who is also the chief executive officer (executive director/CEO). The executive director/CEO, reports to the AMHCA president, manages the staff's work in carrying out AMHCA's strategic plan, manages the resources of the association, and oversees the execution of the decisions made by the board of directors.

Chapter 6: The Organization of the American Mental Health Counselors Association

Organization of AMHCA

AMHCA Board of Directors

Officers of AMHCA
- President
- President-Elect
- Past President
- Treasurer
- Director-at-Large
- Midwest Region Director
- North Atlantic Region Director
- Southern Region Director
- Western Region Director
- Graduate Students and Emerging Professionals Committee Chair
- Executive Director and Chief Executive Officer
- Ex-Officio Members of the Board (liaisons to other associations)

AMHCA's Mission

To advance the profession of clinical mental health counseling by setting the standard for:
- Collaboration
- Advocacy
- Research
- Ethical Practice
- Education, Training, and Professional Development

AMHCA's Vision

To position Clinical Mental Health Counselors to meet the health care needs of those we serve while advancing the profession.

AMHCA State Chapters

AMHCA Standing Committees
- Executive
- Advancement for Clinical Practice
- AMHCA Credentialing Certification Board
- Awards and Recognition
- Annual Conference
- Continuing Education
- Ethics
- Graduate Students and Emerging Professionals
- Public Awareness Public Policy and Legislation
- State Chapter Resource Development

AMHCA Staff
- Executive Director/Chief Executive Officer
- Chief Strategic Officer, and Director of Communications and State Chapter Relations
- Director of Operations, Finance and Membership
- Director of the Office of Credentialing and Continuing Education
- Director of Program Coordination
- Other Supports
  - Editor, *Journal of Clinical Mental Health Counseling*
  - Editor, *The Advocate Magazine* and other AMHCA publications
  - Legislative Advocates

AMHCA Mission and Vision Statements

The mission and vision of AMHCA promote the advocacy of enhanced mental and emotional well-being for all through effective public policy and other initiatives that address integrated behavioral health.

AMHCA's Mission: To advance the profession of clinical mental health counseling by setting the standard for:

- Collaboration
- Advocacy
- Research
- Ethical Practice
- Education, Training, and Professional Development

AMHCA's Vision: To position Clinical Mental Health Counselors to meet the health care needs of those we serve while advancing the profession.

State Chapters

Each AMHCA-chartered state chapter is essential to the success of the association in serving the needs of the members and the profession of clinical mental health counseling. Generally, state chapters are organized similarly to AMHCA's board of directors, and state chapter bylaws typically reflect AMHCA's bylaws. State leaders have wide discrepancy in acting in behalf of the members of the profession within their state.

AMHCA encourages state chapter leaders to allow their members to participate in the AMHCA Unified Dues program. This program affords a 20 percent discount to members who simultaneously join both AMHCA and their state chapter. Not all state chapters participate in this program. For more information see *www.amhca.org/members/joinamhca/unified*.

Members Who Serve in AMHCA

All members of AMHCA who are in good standing may volunteer to serve in any of the association's positions. Vacant positions on the board of directors are proposed by the past president and elected by the members of the association.

The chairs of AMHCA's standing committees are appointed by the AMHCA president and are usually selected from among members who have previously served on the respective AMHCA committees. Committee members are proposed by the standing committee chairs and are often individuals who have volunteered to serve on a given committee.

In most positions, members are LCMHCs who are licensed to practice independently. However, any individual may offer to serve on a committee and in other positions if they are qualified. With the exception of paid full-time staff members, AMHCA is an association run by unpaid volunteers who have a commitment to the profession of clinical mental health counseling.

All interested individuals are encouraged to consider participating in AMHCA's state chapter positions or in positions in the national association. Every member can contribute to the advancement of the profession.

Chapter 6: The Organization of the American Mental Health Counselors Association

Officers of the AMHCA Board of Directors

The association is governed by a board of directors. Most members of the board serve three-year terms. AMHCA holds elections in the spring of each year, during which vacancies are filled. The board comprises these positions:

- *President.* The president is the presiding officer of the board of directors. The president serves for a total of three years, the first year as president-elect, the second year as president, and the third year as past president. The president conducts the association's business and entertains official motions by the other members of the board. The board of directors is guided by *Robert's Rules of Order*. As a voting member and chair of the board of directors, the president leads the association by proposing association initiatives, overseeing the strategic plan, and managing the governance of the association. In addition to other duties, the president appoints committee chairs and serves as the chair of the association's executive committee.

- *President-Elect.* The president-elect votes as a member of the board of directors after being elected by AMHCA's membership. This individual has a primary responsibility to coordinate the preparation of AMHCA's annual conference with the help of board members and a conference planning committee. The president-elect also assists in developing the association's initiatives and is a member of the executive committee.

- *Past President.* After completing two years of service as AMHCA's president-elect and president, the past president continues to work on the association's initiatives as a voting member of the board of directors. The past president has a major responsibility to screen and nominate candidates for positions on the AMHCA board of directors.

- *Treasurer.* The treasurer of the association is elected for a three-year term. As a voting member of the board of directors, the treasurer reports directly to the AMHCA president and the board of directors. Working closely with the executive director/CEO, the treasurer oversees the management of AMHCA's financial resources and supervises fiscal accounting. Because of these responsibilities, the treasurer is also a member of the executive committee.

- *Director-at-Large.* This voting member of the board of directors is responsible for overseeing the important initiatives of the association. Representing all members, the director-at-large brings matters of member interest to the board of directors that will further advance the profession and all LCMHCs. Like the other members of the board of directors, the director-at-large is elected to a three-year term of office.

- *Region Directors.* AMHCA is composed of four regions:
  - North Atlantic Region
  - Southern Region
  - Midwest Region
  - Western Region

  The region directors are voting members of the board of directors who coordinate activities within AMHCA's state chapters in their respective regions. They act as communication channels for AMHCA to the leaders of the state chapters and from these leaders back to AMHCA. They manage the implementation of AMHCA initiatives within the states assigned to their regions. Region directors are elected to three-year-terms.

- *Graduate Students and Emerging Professionals Committee Chair.* The chair of this committee is invited to participate in the meetings of the board of directors. Issues of import to both graduate students and emerging professionals are brought to the attention of the board for discussion and appropriate action. The chair of this committee is a voting member of the board.

- *Executive Director and Chief Executive Officer.* The executive director/CEO, is a voting member of the board and is responsible for executing board decisions. Reporting directly to the president and the board of directors, the executive director/CEO, represents the other members of the AMHCA staff.

- *Ex-Officio Members of the Board.* The AMHCA board of directors includes *ex-officio* members who represent the association in various responsibilities. These individuals typically serve as liaisons to other associations. They keep the president and other members of the board of directors informed of initiatives and the need for coordination. *Ex-officio* members are appointed by the AMHCA board of directors. They participate in board discussions but cannot vote on any motion.

The Standing Committees of AMHCA

The association's standing committees play a vital role in advancing the interests of AMHCA's members and in promoting the profession of clinical mental health counseling.

- *Executive Committee.* The Executive Committee is presided over by the president, who entertains motions that will be advanced to the board of directors for official approval. This committee also oversees the accountability of the AMHCA executive director/CEO. In addition to the president, voting members of the committee include the president-elect, past president, treasurer, and executive director/CEO.

- *Advancement for Clinical Practice Committee* (formerly the Professional Development Committee). This committee considers all career and professional advancement initiatives that impact the profession of clinical mental health counseling. The committee actively manages and revises *AMHCA Standards for the Practice of Clinical Mental Health Counseling.* This document has been the cornerstone reference for the profession since 1979 and has been used to justify federal hiring and reimbursement. In addition to the *AMHCA Standards,* the committee promotes professional initiatives (e.g., writes AMHCA Clinical Practice Briefs), coordinates with other standing committees, and makes proposals to the board of directors.

- *AMHCA Credentialing Certification Board (formerly the AMHCA Diplomate Committee).* This board is responsible for reviewing and approving the advanced practice certifications. These certifications include the AMHCA Clinical Mental Health Counseling Specialist, AMHCA Diplomate in Advanced Clinical Mental Health Counseling Practice, and AMHCA Fellow in Clinical Mental Health Counseling Education and Research. The director of the AMHCA Credentialing Certification Board supervises the application process and assigns board members to assess and qualify applications. Each application is independently reviewed by at least three board members.

- *Awards and Recognition Committee.* Every year, the association recognizes a number of professionals who have contributed to the profession. It also makes other awards for state chapters. This committee manages these awards. Nominations are solicited each spring, the nominees are vetted, and selections for the awards are announced at AMHCA's annual conference.

- *Annual Conference Committee.* Each year, AMHCA conducts a conference for professional development. Prior to the annual conference, AMHCA also hosts Leadership Training for state chapter leaders. The chair of the Conference Planning Committee is the president-elect. The committee is engaged in selecting presenters, organizing the many details of the conference, and the training of state leaders.

- *Continuing Education Committee.* The CEC Mission is to ensure the highest possible quality for AMHCA training programs and educational opportunities for professionals in the clinical mental health counseling profession. The CEC's goal is to provide AMHCA members with a planned system of high-quality continuing education programs designed and delivered to enhance attainment and retention of technical competence by clinical mental health counselors.

Chapter 6: The Organization of the American Mental Health Counselors Association

- *Ethics Committee.* This committee's primary responsibility is to oversee the *AMHCA Code of Ethics.* As circumstances warrant, members of the Ethics Committee review the provisions of the *Code* and amend it when needed. The committee deliberates the ethical issues of AMHCA's members and considers the codes of ethics of other mental health professional associations. It is continuously focused on improving the *AMHCA Code of Ethics* to reflect the profession's concerns for ethical clinical practice.

- *The Graduate Students and Emerging Professionals Committee.* This committee represents the interests of graduate students in clinical mental health counseling master's degree programs and doctoral programs in Counselor Education and Supervision. It also represents the interests of recently graduated counselors who are not yet licensed to practice independently without supervision. The chair of the committee supervises the activities and initiatives of graduate students and emerging professionals and acts as the committee's primary liaison to the AMHCA board of directors.

- *Public Awareness Committee.* This committee is responsible for increasing public consciousness about the clinical mental health counseling profession. In addition, the committee sponsors initiatives of general import regarding mental health issues and the public education of mental and emotional well-being.

- *Public Policy and Legislation Committee.* AMHCA represents the interests of the profession and its members to the U.S. Congress with other allied associations. The association also monitors state legislation and public policy that is significant to AMHCA's objectives. This committee works to promote mental health initiatives at both the state and national levels of government regarding the laws and regulations that impact the profession of clinical mental health counseling as well as the welfare of the public.

- *State Chapter Resource Development Committee.* AMHCA is the sponsoring association for state chapters located throughout the United States and the District of Columbia. The chair of this committee provides liaison to the AMHCA's region directors. The committee proposes initiatives that will further the interests of the state chapters and their members.

The AMHCA Staff

The association's day-to-day operations are conducted by members of the AMHCA staff, who fulfill the policies of the board of directors. The AMHCA phone number is (703) 548–6002. For each staff director's email address, visit *www.amhca.org/about/about-us/aboutamhca/staff.*

- *Executive Director/Chief Executive Officer.* The day-to-day management of the association is the responsibility of the executive director/CEO. This staff member directs all of the activities of the members of the AMHCA staff. Reporting directly to the president and the board of directors, the executive director/CEO is also a voting member of the board. The executive director/CEO also plays a crucial role in legislative advocacy at the national level.

- *Chief Strategic Officer, and Director of Communications and State Chapter Relations.* This staff director oversees technology and is responsible for all of the association's media communications. In addition, this director coordinates with state chapters and with the chair of the State Chapter Resource Development Committee.

- *Director of Operations, Finance and Membership:* This staff director oversees all of the association's financial functions; directs its financial policies, planning, reporting, and controls; and establishes strategies to maintain its financial stability. In addition to developing procedures and policies for the association's administration, the director organizes membership activities, developments, and relations; maintains the membership database; and administers AMHCA's member recruitment and retention program.

- *Director of the Office of Credentialing and Continuing Education (OCCE).* This staff director provides staff approval of applications for AMHCA-approved CEs and expert trainers. This director also manages credentialing and coordinates with the director of the AMHCA Credentialing Certification Board and the CE Committee.

- *Director of Program Coordination.* This director coordinates the work of the AMHCA standing committees in accordance with guidance from the executive director/CEO and the board of directors. Because the initiatives of the several committees often require synchronization among the committee chairs, this director assists in these actions.

- In support of AMHCA's mission, several additional individuals supplement the work of AMHCA's staff. These include the editor and production manager of the *Journal of Clinical Mental Health Counseling (JMHC)*, the editor of *The Advocate Magazine* and other AMHCA publications, and legislative advocates for the U.S. Congress.

Strategic Plan

AMHCA operates in accordance with its bylaws, policies, and strategic plan. This plan is periodically updated to reflect the current goals of AMHCA's board of directors. It includes the operational priorities of the association and provides functional directions to the executive director/CEO.

AMHCA Publications

The following AMHCA publications can be found under the Publications tab at *www.amhca.org*:

- *The Clinical Mental Health Counselor Declaration: A Hippocratic Pledge* (Appendix G): In concert with the AMHCA Code of Ethics, The *Declaration* was developed as a public commitment by members of the profession to serve others with honor and integrity.

- *AMHCA Standards for the Practice of Clinical Mental Health Counseling* (Appendix B): The standards serve as a framework for the specific knowledge and skills of the profession.

- *AMHCA Code of Ethics* (Appendix C): *AMHCA Code of Ethics* is a detailed and thorough description of applied ethical practice.

- *Journal of Clinical Mental Counseling: JMHC* is a scholarly, peer-reviewed journal regarding research and other topics relevant to the profession that is printed quarterly.

- *The Advocate Magazine:* This printed periodical highlights current subjects of interest to members of the profession.

- Other AMHCA publications, including Practice Guidelines, Position Papers, etc., are available at *www.amhca.org/publications*.

CHAPTER 7

Other Organizations and Associations Related to Counseling

Exploring How Organizations Influence Mental Health

"If you want to improve the organization, you have to improve yourself and the organization gets pulled up with you. That is a big lesson. I cannot just expect the organization to improve if I don't improve myself and lift the organization."

Indra Nooyi

What are the relationships among the American Mental Health Counselors Association (AMHCA) and other organizations?

Many who are new to clinical mental health counseling are amazed by the number of acronyms used within the profession. Many of these acronyms reference other associations or organizations that relate to counseling. The charts below describe some of these key organizations:

- ❑ Professional associations
- ❑ Accrediting organizations
- ❑ Counseling-related organizations
- ❑ Other related organizations

These lists are not exhaustive. For organizations that have not been included, please consult an online search engine.

Professional Associations

AAMFT	American Association for Marriage and Family Therapy *www.aamft.org*
	AAMFT is a professional association in the field of marriage and family therapy. It represents licensed Marriage and Family Therapists throughout the United States, Canada, and abroad.
ACA	American Counseling Association *www.counseling.org*
	ACA is an association that encompasses all categories of counseling. This association has divisions that represent vocational rehabilitation counseling, guidance counseling, college counseling, counseling educators, humanistic counseling, etc. ACA places a strong emphasis on social justice. Since 1998, AMHCA and the American School Counselor Association (ASCA) have been legally independent associations; however, they were also ACA-affiliated divisions. As of 2019, both AMHCA and ASCA are disaffiliated with ACA, but they still work together on initiatives of mutual interest.
ACES	Association for Counseling Education and Supervision *www.acesonline.net*
	ACES is a division of ACA dedicated to quality education and supervision of counselors in all work settings. ACES members are counselors, supervisors, graduate students, and faculty members who strive to improve the education and supervision of counselors in training and in practice.

Chapter 7: Other Organizations and Associations Related to Counseling

APA	American Psychiatric Association *www.psychiatry.org* The American Psychiatric Association is the professional organization of psychiatrists and trainee psychiatrists in the United States. The association publishes many journals and pamphlets, as well as the "Diagnostic and Statistical Manual of Mental Disorders" (DSM), which is used as a guide for diagnosing disorders.
APA	American Psychological Association *www.apa.org* APA is the leading scientific and professional psychology organization in the United States, representing members who are researchers, educators, clinicians, consultants, and students. APA promotes the advancement, communication, and application of psychological science and knowledge to benefit society and improve lives.
ASCA	American School Counselor Association *www.schoolcounselor.org* Founded in 1952, the American School Counselor Association is an association that works to meets the needs of all school counselors, regardless of setting, experience level, or needs. With a membership of school counseling professionals from around the world, ASCA focuses on providing professional development, enhancing school counseling programs, and researching effective school counseling practices.
CAMFT	California Association of Marriage and Family Therapists *www.camft.org* CAMFT is an independent professional organization representing the interests of licensed Marriage and Family Therapists in California and is not a division of AAMFT. It is dedicated to maintaining high standards of professional ethics, to upholding the qualifications of the profession, and to expanding awareness of the profession.
NASW	National Association of Social Workers *www.socialworkers.org* NASW is a professional organization of Social Workers in the United States. The association provides guidance, research, up-to-date information, advocacy, and other resources for its members and for Social Workers in general.

Accrediting Organizations

| CACREP | The Council for Accreditation of Counseling & Related Educational Programs
www.cacrep.org

CACREP is the federally recognized accreditor of counseling programs in the United States. It accredits both master's and doctoral degree counseling programs including master's degree programs in Clinical Mental Health Counseling, other master's degree programs, and doctoral degree programs in Counselor Education and Supervision. |
|---|---|
| MPCAC | Masters in Psychology and Counseling Accreditation Council
www.mpcacaccreditation.org

MPCAC is an independent counseling association that is not affiliated with the American Psychological Association. The accreditation provided by this council is not currently recognized by the federal government. Therefore, those who graduate from MPCAC-accredited master's programs may not be employed by federal agencies, and may not be eligible for some forms of federal reimbursement. |

Counseling-Related Organizations

| AASCB | American Association of State Counseling Boards
www.aascb.org

AASCB is the organization of state boards that regulate the practice of counseling. Founded in 1985, it is the resource for information about counselor licensing and regulation, test development, and standards for licensing. |
|---|---|
| NBCC | National Board for Certified Counselors, Inc. and Affiliates
www.nbcc.org

NBCC is an international certifying organization for counselors. It is an independent, not-for-profit credentialing organization. The purpose of the organization is to establish and monitor a certification system for counselors and to identify and maintain a register of certified counselors. NBCC offers several certifications. It also offers testing to certify counselors through the National Counselor Examination (NCE) as well as the National Clinical Mental Health Counseling Examination (NCMHCE) that originated with AMHCA. For counselors, the two most common certifications are National Certified Counselor (NCC) and Certified Clinical Mental Health Counselor (CCMHC). |

Chapter 7: Other Organizations and Associations Related to Counseling

Other Related Organizations

NAMI	National Alliance on Mental Illness *www.nami.org* NAMI is an advocacy group originally founded as a grassroots group by family members of people diagnosed with mental disorders. NAMI identifies its mission as "dedicated to building better lives for the millions of Americans affected by mental illness."
NIMH	National Institute of Mental Health *www.nimh.nih.gov* NIMH is one of the 27 institutes and centers that make up the National Institutes of Health (NIH). The NIH is an agency of the U. S. Department of Health and Human Services and is the primary agency of the U.S. government responsible for biomedical and health-related research. NIMH is the largest research organization in the world that specializes in mental illness.
SAMHSA	Substance Abuse and Mental Health Services Administration *www.samhsa.gov.* SAMHSA is the federal agency within the U.S. Department of Health and Human Services that leads public health efforts to advance the behavioral health of the nation. SAMHSA's mission is to reduce the impact of substance use and mental illness on America's communities.

APPENDIXES

APPENDIX A

AMHCA's Mission and Vision Statements

The mission and vision of AMHCA promote the advocacy of enhanced mental and emotional well-being for all through effective public policy and other initiatives that enrich integrated behavioral health.

AMHCA's Mission

To advance the profession of clinical mental health counseling by setting the standard for:

- Collaboration
- Advocacy
- Research
- Ethical Practice
- Education, Training, and Professional Development

AMHCA's Vision

To position Clinical Mental Health Counselors to meet the health care needs of those we serve while advancing the profession.

For more information about AMHCA, visit *www.amhca.org/about/about-us*.

APPENDIX B

AMHCA Standards for the Practice of Clinical Mental Health Counseling

The Essential Standards for the
Art and Science of the Profession

How are the *AMHCA Standards* applied in practice?

The American Mental Health Counselors Association's *Standards for the Practice of Clinical Mental Counseling (AMHCA Standards)* specifies the established benchmarks of practice for members of the clinical mental health counseling profession. As noted throughout "Essentials of the Clinical Mental Health Counseling Profession," the acronym LCMHC is used to refer to all categories of clinical mental health counselors. These categories include Clinical Mental Health Counseling Students (CMHC Students) in supervised internships, postgraduate Supervised Clinical Mental Health Counselors (Supervised CMHCs), and fully Licensed Clinical Mental Health Counselors (LCMHCs). Regardless of graduate-degree program title or state license title, *AMHCA Standards for the Practice of Clinical Mental Health Counseling* provides professional development standards for each of the clinical mental health counselor categories.

AMHCA Standards identifies and describes the norms within the profession. The standards spelled out in this important document have served as the foundation of the profession since 1979, when they were first adopted. *AMHCA Standards* has been periodically revised and extended as the profession developed. In the past, the explicit requirements for practice, education, and supervision were used to validate clinical mental health counselor qualifications as one of the four recognized mental health professions (the other three are psychology, social work, and marriage and family therapy).

The National Academy of Medicine (formerly the Institute of Medicine) in its 2010 report cited the *AMHCA Standards* for members of the profession to be eligible and qualified for federal employment and reimbursement, saying in its first recommendation: "Independent practice of mental health counselors in TRICARE in the circumstances in which their education, licensure, and clinical experience have helped to prepare them to diagnose, and where appropriate, treat conditions in the beneficiary population" ("Provision of Mental Health Counseling Services Under TRICARE," Chapter 6, page 207, at *bit.ly/2qqYyxP*).

AMHCA Standards is a living document that is updated on a continuing basis to meet the needs of the public and the profession. In addition to standards of practice, it includes training and supervision standards.

Of special note are the specific clinical mental health counseling knowledge and skills. Specific standards fall into the following two categories:

1. Standards that LCMHCs should be familiar with:

    - Biological Bases of Behavior
    - Specialized Clinical Assessment
    - Substance Use Disorders and Co-occurring Disorders
    - Technology Supported Counseling and Communications (TSCC)
    - Trauma-Informed Care

2. Standards that LCMHCs who specialize in one or more specialist areas should have in order to comprehensively apply the knowledge and skills in practice. Areas of clinical specialization include:

    - Aging and Older Adults Standards and Competencies
    - Biological Bases of Behavior
    - Child and Adolescent Standards and Competencies
    - Integrated Behavioral Health Care Counseling
    - Specialized Clinical Assessment
    - Substance Use Disorders and Co-occurring Disorders
    - Technology Supported Counseling and Communications (TSCC)
    - Trauma-Informed Care

    Note that the standards for both Trauma-Informed Care as well as Substance Use Disorders and Co-occurring Disorders are listed in both categories. LCMHCs who specialize in these or the other specialist areas should possess a superior, in-depth understanding of the knowledge and skills that is applied in practice.

    The need is expanding for mental health professionals who have advanced, postgraduate training and experience in treating populations with special needs. AMHCA's Advancement for Clinical Practice Committee has been at the forefront of identifying the knowledge and skills required for members of the clinical mental health counseling profession to become specialists.

The 2020 version of the *AMHCA Standards*—published in this edition of "Essentials of the Clinical Mental Health Counseling Profession" and online at *www.amhca.org/publications/standards* is the first comprehensive update to the *AMHCA Standards* since the 2012 version. AMHCA's Advancement for Clinical Practice Committee (ACPC) reports that the 2020 version includes two revised and updated standards, and four new standards that have been developed since 2012.

The two revised and updated standards are:

Appendix B: *AMHCA Standards for the Practice of Clinical Mental Health Counseling*

- Substance Use Disorders and Co-occurring Disorders, which was Co-occurring Disorders in 2012
- Trauma-Informed Care, which was Trauma Training Standards in 2012

The four entirely new standards that have been added to the latest edition of the *AMHCA Standards* are:

- Technology Supported Counseling and Communications (TSCC), which was originally published as Technology Assisted Counseling (TAC)
- Integrated Behavioral Health Care Counseling
- Aging and Older Adults Standards and Competencies
- Child and Adolescent Standards and Competencies

The AMHCA board and the ACPC have begun working on a new standard—Forensic Evaluation—that will specify the knowledge and skill competencies related to forensic evaluation. The forensic standard will likely be approved in 2020. Other need-based competencies that have been identified as future standards are under development and will be included in future publications and distribution. These include Military Counseling, Couples and Family Counseling, and Developmental and Learning Disabilities Counseling, etc.

This unabridged version of the latest *AMHCA Standards for the Practice of Clinical Mental Health Counseling* appears here in Appendix B, and is also downloadable at no cost from *www.amhca.org/publications/standards*.

AMHCA Standards for the Practice of Clinical Mental Health Counseling

Adopted 1979

Revised 1992, 1993, 1999, 2003, 2011, 2015, 2016, 2017, 2018, and 2020

I. Introduction

  A. Scope of Practice

  B. Standards of Practice and Research

II. Educational and Pre-Degree Clinical Training Standards

  A. Program

  B. Curriculum

  C. Specialized Clinical Mental Health Counseling Training

  D. Pre-degree Clinical Mental Health Counseling Field Work Guidelines

III. Faculty and Supervisor Standards

  A. Faculty Standards

  B. Supervisor Standards

IV. Clinical Practice Standards

  A. Post-Degree/Pre-Licensure

  B. Peer Review and Supervision

  C. Continuing Education

  D. Legal and Ethical Issues

V. Recommend AMHCA Training

  A. Biological Bases of Behavior

  B. Specialized Clinical Assessment

  C. Trauma-Informed Care

  D. Substance Use Disorders and Co-occurring Disorders

  E. Technology Supported Counseling and Communications (TSCC), which was originally published as Technology Assisted Counseling (TAC)

  F. Integrated Behavioral Health Care Counseling

  G. Child and Adolescent Standards and Competencies

  H. Aging and Older Adults Standards and Competencies

Appendix B: AMHCA Standards for the Practice of Clinical Mental Health Counseling

I. Introduction

Since its formation as a professional organization in 1976, the American Mental Health Counselors Association, AMHCA, has been committed to establishing and promoting vigorous standards for education and training, professional practice, and professional ethics for clinical mental health counselors. Initially, AMHCA sought to define and promote the professional identity of mental health counselors. Today, with licensure laws in all 50 states, AMHCA strives to enhance the practice of clinical mental health counseling and to promote standards for clinical education and clinical practice that anticipate the future roles of clinical mental health counselors within the broader health care system. As a professional association, AMHCA affiliated with APGA (a precursor to the American Counseling Association [ACA]) as a division in 1978; in 1998, AMHCA became a separate not-for-profit organization, but retained its status as a division of ACA.

In 1976, a group of community mental health, community agency and private practice counselors founded AMHCA as the professional association for the newly emerging group of counselors who identified their practice as "mental health counseling." Without credentialing, licensure, education and training standards, or other marks of a clinical profession, these early mental health counselors worked alongside social workers and psychologists in the developing community mental health service system as "paraprofessionals" or "allied health professionals" despite the fact that they held master's or doctoral degrees. By 1979, the early founders of AMHCA had organized four key mechanisms for defining the new clinical professional specialty:

1. Identifying a definition of mental health counseling
2. Setting standards for education and training, clinical practice, and professional ethics
3. Creating a national credentialing system
4. Starting a professional journal, which included research and clinical practice content

These mechanisms have significantly contributed to the professional development of clinical mental health counseling and merit further explication.

A. Scope of Practice

A crucial development in mental health counseling has been defining the roles and functions of the profession. The initial issue of AMHCA's *Journal of Mental Health Counseling* included the first published definition of mental health counseling as "an interdisciplinary, multifaceted, holistic process of: 1) the promotion of healthy lifestyles; 2) identification of individual stressors and personal levels of functioning; and 3) the preservation or restoration of mental health" (Seiler & Messina, 1979).

In 1986, the AMHCA board of directors adopted a more formal, comprehensive definition: "Clinical mental health counseling is the provision of professional counseling services involving the application of principles of psychotherapy, human development, learning theory, group dynamics, and the etiology of mental illness and dysfunctional behavior to individuals, couples, families and groups, for the purpose of promoting optimal mental health, dealing with normal problems of living and treating psychopathology. The practice of clinical mental health counseling includes, but is not limited to, diagnosis and treatment of mental and emotional disorders, psycho-educational techniques aimed at the prevention of mental and emotional disorders, consultations to individuals, couples, families, groups, organizations and communities, and clinical research into more effective psychotherapeutic treatment modalities."

Clinical mental health counselors have always understood that their professional work encompasses a broad range of clinical practice, including dealing with normal problems of living and promoting optimal mental health in addition to the prevention, intervention and treatment of mental and emotional disorders. This work of clinical mental health counselors serves the needs of socially and culturally diverse clients (e.g., age, gender, race/ ethnicity, socioeconomic status, sexual orientation, etc.) across the life span (i.e. children, adolescents and adults including older adults and geriatric populations). Clinical mental health counselors have developed a strong sense of professional identity since 1976. AMHCA has sought to support this sense of professional identity through legislative and professional advocacy, professional standards, a code of ethics, continuing education, and clinical educational resources, and support for evidence based best practices, research and peer-reviewed dissemination of developments in the field.

B. Standards of Practice and Research

A key development for the profession was AMHCA's creation of education and training standards for mental health counselors in 1979. The Council for Accreditation of Counseling & Related Educational Programs (CACREP) adopted and adapted these AMHCA training standards in 1988 when it established the first set of accreditation standards for master's programs in clinical mental health counseling. In keeping with AMHCA standards, CACREP accreditation standards for the mental health counseling specialty have consistently required 60 semester hours of graduate coursework. AMHCA remained an active advocate for vigorous clinical training standards through the 2009 CACREP accreditation standards revision process, during which community counseling accreditation standards were merged into the new clinical mental health counseling standards. After careful review, AMHCA endorsed the clinical mental health counseling standards.

Another important step in the further professionalization of clinical mental health counseling, AMHCA established the National Academy of Certified Mental Health Counselors, the first credentialing body for clinical mental health counselors, and gave its first certification examination in 1979. In 1993, this certified clinical mental health counselor credential (CCMHC) was transferred to the National Board for Certified Counselors (NBCC). NBCC provides the Board Certification of CCMHCs. AMHCA clinical standards have always recognized and incorporated the CCMHC credential as an important means of recognizing that a clinical mental health counselor has met independent clinical practice standards, despite significant differences that exist among state counselor licensure laws, as well as among educational and training programs.

Finally, since 1979, AMHCA published the *Journal of Mental Health Counseling,* which has become widely recognized and cited as an important contributor to the research and professional literature on clinical mental health counseling.

Taken together, these four mechanisms (definition of scope of practice; educational and training standards, professional practice standards and code of ethics; credentialing; and professional journal) resulted in the recognition of clinical mental health counseling as an important profession to be included in our health care system. In recognition of the central importance of vigorous professional educational and clinical practice standards, AMHCA has periodically revised its professional standards in 1993-94, 1999, 2003, and 2010-11 to reflect evolving practice requirements. These professional standards, as well as the 2015 *AMHCA Code of Ethics,* constitute the basis from which AMHCA continues to advocate for, and seek to advance, the practice of clinical mental health counseling.

II. Educational and Pre-Degree Clinical Training Standards

Required Education: Master's in Clinical Mental Health Counseling (60 semester hours)

A. Program

CACREP-accredited clinical mental health counseling program—based on 2009 standards (endorsed by AMHCA Board) or master's degree in counseling (minimum of 48 semester hours) from a regionally accredited institution. The 48 semester-hour minimum will increase to 60 semester hours in January 2016.

B. Curriculum

Consistent with 2009 *CACREP Standards,* clinical mental health counseling programs should include the core CACREP areas and specialized training in clinical mental health counseling. The core CACREP areas include:

1. Professional Orientation and Ethical Practice
2. Social and Cultural Diversity
3. Human Growth and Development Across the Life Span
4. Career Development
5. Counseling Theories and Helping Relationships
6. Group Work
7. Assessment
8. Research and Program Evaluation

C. Specialized Clinical Mental Health Counseling Training:

These areas of clinical mental health counselor preparation address the clinical mental health needs across the life span (children, adolescents, adults and older adults) and across socially and culturally diverse populations:

1. Ethical, Legal and Practice Foundations of Clinical Mental Health Counseling
2. Prevention and Clinical Intervention
3. Clinical Assessment
4. Diagnosis and Treatment of Mental Disorders
5. Diversity and Advocacy in Clinical Mental Health Counseling
6. Clinical Mental Health Counseling Research and Outcome Evaluation

AMHCA recommends additional training in Clinical Mental Health Counseling described in the following standards:

1. Biological Bases of Behavior (including psychopathology and psychopharmacology)
2. Trauma-Informed Care

3. Substance Use Disorders and Co-occurring Disorders (generally refers to addictions and accompanying mental disorders)

This training may be completed as part of the degree program, in post-master's coursework, or as part of a certificate or continuing education or CCMHC credential.

D. Pre-Degree Clinical Mental Health Counseling Field Work Guidelines

1. Students' pre-degree clinical experiences meet the minimum training standards of 100 Practicum and 600 Internship hours.

2. Students receive an hour of clinical supervision by an independently and approved licensed supervisor for every 20 hours of client direct care. This field work supervision is in addition to the practicum and internship requirements for their academic program.

3. Students are individually supervised by a supervisor with no more than 6 (FTE) or 12 total supervisees.

III. Faculty and Supervisor Standards

A. Faculty Standards

Faculty with primary responsibility for clinical mental health counseling programs should have an earned doctorate in a field related to clinical mental health counseling and identify with the field of clinical mental health counseling. While AMHCA recognizes that clinical mental health counseling programs have the need for diverse non-primary faculty who may not meet all of the following criteria, the following knowledge and skills are required for faculty with primary responsibility for clinical mental health counseling programs.

1. **Knowledge**
    a. Demonstrate expertise in the content areas in which they teach and have a thorough understanding of client populations served.
    b. Involved in clinical supervision either as instructors or in the field have a working knowledge of current supervision models and apply them to the supervisory process.
    c. Understand that clinical mental health counselors are asked to provide a range of services including counseling clients about problems of living, promoting optimal mental health, and treatment of mental and emotional disorders across the life span.
    d. Demonstrate training in the following:
        i. Evidence-based best practices
        ii. Differential diagnosis and treatment planning
        iii. Co-occurring disorders and substance use disorders
        iv. Trauma, and its related forms (developmental, complex, situation, chronic or toxic distress, family generational trauma, historical trauma, etc.)
        v. Biological bases of behavior including psychopharmacology
        vi. Social and cultural foundations of behavior

Appendix B: AMHCA Standards for the Practice of Clinical Mental Health Counseling

---

      vii. Individual family and group counseling

      viii. Clinical assessment and testing

      ix. Professional orientation and ethics

      x. Advocacy and leadership

      xi. Case consultation and supervision with peers or specialists

      xii. Clinical supervision with a hierarchical or regulatory supervisor

  e. Possess knowledge about professional boundaries as well as professional behavior in all interactions with students and colleagues.

2. **Skills**

    a. Demonstrate clinical mental health skills by completing licensure requirements including successful completion of coursework, fieldwork requirements, licensure exams, and licensure renewal requirements.

    b. Demonstrate identification with the field of clinical mental health counseling by their academic credentials, scholarship and professional affiliations including their participation in organizations which promote clinical mental health counseling including AMHCA, ACA and ACES etc. Faculty who provide clinical supervision in the program or on site are able to lead supervision seminars which promote case analysis, small group process and critical thinking.

    c. Complete the equivalent of 15 semester hours of coursework at the doctoral level in the clinical mental health specialty area or a comparable amount of scholarship in this area.

    d. Possess expertise in working with diverse client populations in areas they teach including clients across the spectrum of social class, ethnic/racial groups, lesbian, gay, bisexual and transgendered communities, etc.

    e. Demonstrate and model the ability to develop and maintain clear role boundaries within the teaching relationship.

    f. Demonstrate the ability to analyze and evaluate skills and performance of students.

B. **Supervisor Standards**

AMHCA recommends at least 24 continuing education hours or equivalent graduate credit hours of training in the theory and practice of clinical supervision for those clinical mental health counselors who provide pre- or post-degree clinical supervision to clinical mental health counseling students or trainees. AMHCA recommends that clinical supervisors obtain, on the average, at least 3 continuing education hours in supervision per year as part of their overall program of continuing education. Clinical supervisors should meet the following knowledge and skills criteria.

1. **Knowledge**

    a. Possess a strong working knowledge of evidence based and best practices orientation with clinical theory and interventions and application to the clinical process.

    b. Understand the client population and the practice setting of the supervisee.

    c. Understand and have a working knowledge of current supervision models and their application to the supervisory process. Maintain a working knowledge of the most current methods and techniques in clinical supervision knowledge of group supervision methodology including the appropriate use and limits of this modality.

 d. Identify and understand the roles, functions and responsibilities of clinical supervisors including liability in the supervisory process. Communicates expectations and nature and extent of the supervision relationship.

 e. Maintain a working knowledge of appropriate professional development activities for supervisees. These activities should be focused on empirically based scientific knowledge.

 f. Show a strong understanding of the supervisory relationship and related issues, not limited to power differential, evaluation, parallel process and isomorphic similarities and differences between supervision and counseling, and qualities that enhance the supervisor/supervisee working alliance for the benefit of clients served.

 g. Identify and define the cultural issues that arise in clinical supervision and be able to routinely incorporate cultural sensitivity into the supervisory process.

 h. Understand and define the legal and ethical issues in clinical supervision including:

  i. Applicable laws, licensure rules, and the *AMHCA Code of Ethics,* specifically as they relate to supervision

  ii. Supervisory liability, respondent superior, and fiduciary responsibility

  iii. Risk-management models and processes as they relate to the clinical process and to supervision

 i. Possess a working understanding of the evaluation process in clinical supervision including evaluating supervisee competence and remediation of supervisee skill development. This includes initial, formative and summative assessment of supervisee knowledge, skills and self-awareness with provisions for clearly stated expectations, fair delivery of feedback and due process. Supervision includes both formal and informal feedback mechanisms.

 j. Maintain a working knowledge of industry recognized financial management processes and required recordkeeping practices including electronic records and transmission of records.

2. **Skills**

 a. Possess a thorough understanding and experience in working with the supervisees' client populations. Be able to demonstrate and explain the counselor role and appropriate clinical interventions within the cultural and clinical context.

 b. Develop, maintain and explain the supervision contract to manage supervisee relationships with clear expectations including:

  i. Frequency, location, length, and duration of supervision meetings

  ii. Supervision models and expectations of the supervisee and the supervisor

  iii. Liability and fiduciary responsibility of the supervisor

  iv. The evaluation process, instruments used, and frequency of evaluation

  v. Emergency and critical incident procedures

 c. Demonstrate and model the ability to develop and maintain clear role boundaries and an appropriate balance between consultation and training within the supervisory relationship.

 d. Demonstrate the ability to analyze and evaluate skills and performance of supervisees including the ability to confront and correct unsuitable actions and interventions on the part of the supervisees. Provide timely substantive and formative feedback to supervisees, along with providing cumulative feedback and to train supervisees in techniques and methods in self-appraisal.

e. Present strong problem-solving and dilemma resolution skills and practice skills with supervisees.

f. Develop and demonstrate the ability to implement risk management strategies.

g. Practice and model self-assessment.

h. Seek consultation as needed.

i. Conceptualize cultural differences in therapy and in supervision. Incorporate and model this understanding into the supervisory process.

j. Possess an understanding of group supervision techniques and the role of group supervision in the supervision process.

k. Comply with applicable federal, state, and local law. Take responsibility for supervisees' actions, which include an understanding of recordkeeping and financial management rules and practice.

IV. Clinical Practice Standards

A. Post-Degree/Pre-Licensure

Clinical mental health counselors have a minimum of 3,000 hours of supervised clinical practice post-degree over a period of at least two years. In the process of acquiring the first 3,000 hours of client direct and indirect contact in postgraduate clinical experience, AMHCA recommends a ratio of one hour of supervision for every 20 hours of on-site work hours with a combination of individual, triadic and group supervision.

B. Peer Review and Supervision

Clinical mental health counselors maintain a program of peer review, supervision and consultation even after they are independently licensed. It is expected that clinical mental health counselors seek additional supervision or consultation to respond to the needs of individual clients, as difficulties beyond their range of expertise arise. While need is to be determined individually, independently licensed clinical mental health counselors must ensure an optimal level of consultation and supervision to meet client needs.

C. Continuing Education

Clinical mental health counselors at the post-degree and independently licensed level must comply with state regulations, certification and credentialing requirements to obtain and maintain continuing educational requirements related to the practice of clinical mental health counseling. Clinical mental health counselors maintain a repertoire of specialized counseling skills and participate in continuing education to enhance their knowledge of the practice of clinical mental health counseling.

In accordance with state law, AMHCA recommends that in order to acquire, maintain and enhance skills, counselors actively participate in a formal professional development and continuing education program. This formal professional development ordinarily addresses peer review and consultation, continuum of care, best practices and evidence-based research; advocacy; counselor self-care and impairment, and the *AMHCA Code of Ethics*. Clinical mental health counselors who are involved in independent clinical practice also receive ongoing training relating to independent practice management, accessibility, accurate representation, office procedures, service environment, and reimbursement for services.

D. Legal and Ethical Issues

Clinical mental health counselors who deliver clinical services comply with state statutes and regulations governing the practice of clinical mental health counseling. Clinical mental health counselors adhere to all state laws governing the practice of clinical mental health counseling. In addition, they adhere to all administrative rules, ethical standards, and other requirements of state clinical mental health counseling or other regulatory boards. Counselors obtain competent legal advice concerning compliance with all relevant statutes and regulations. Where state laws lack governing the practice of counseling, counselors strictly adhere to the national standards of care and ethics codes for the clinical practice of mental health counseling and obtain competent legal advice concerning compliance with these standards.

Clinical mental health counselors who deliver clinical services comply with the codes of ethics specific to the practice of clinical mental health counseling. *AMHCA Code of Ethics* outlines behavior which must be adhered to regarding commitment to clients; counselor-client relationship; counselor responsibility and integrity; assessment and diagnosis; recordkeeping, fee arrangements and bartering; consultant and advocate roles; commitment to other professionals; commitment to students, supervisees and employee relationships.

Clinical mental health counselors are first responsible to society, second to consumers, third to the profession, and last to themselves. Clinical mental health counselors identify themselves as members of the counseling profession. They adhere to the codes of ethics mandated by state boards regulating counseling and by the clinical organizations in which they hold membership and certification. They also adhere to ethical standards endorsed by state boards regulating counseling, and cooperate fully with the adjudication procedures of ethics committees, peer review teams, and state boards. All clinical mental health counselors willingly participate in a formal review of their clinical work, as needed. They provide clients appropriate information on filing complaints alleging unethical behavior and respond in a timely manner to a client request to review records.

Of particular concern to AMHCA is that clinical mental health counselors who deliver clinical services respond in a professional manner to all who seek their services. Clinical mental health counselors provide services to each client requesting services regardless of lifestyle, origin, race, color, age, handicap, sex, religion, or sexual orientation. They are knowledgeable and sensitive to cultural diversity and the multicultural issues of clients. Counselors have a duty to acquire the knowledge, skills, and resources to assist diverse clients. If, after seeking increased knowledge and supervision, counselors are still unable to meet the needs of a particular client, they do what is necessary to put the client in contact with an appropriate mental health resource.

V. Recommended AMHCA Training

In addition to the generally agreed on courses and curricula endorsed by the Council for Accreditation of Counseling & Related Educational Programs (CACREP), AMHCA recommends that all Licensed Clinical Mental Health Counselors have specialized training as well as basic knowledge and skills in the following subject areas:

Appendix B: AMHCA Standards for the Practice of Clinical Mental Health Counseling

- ❑ Biological Bases of Behavior
- ❑ Specialized Clinical Assessment
- ❑ Trauma-Informed Care
- ❑ Substance Use Disorders and Co-occurring Disorders
- ❑ Technology Supported Counseling and Communications
- ❑ Integrated behavioral health care counseling
- ❑ Working With Children and Adolescents
- ❑ Working With Older Persons

In graduate school, knowledge and skills related to any of the above subject areas may be covered in a single course, or more commonly, across several courses or topics of inquiry.

Further, Supervised CMHCs and LCMHCs are encouraged to obtain post-master's training. For example, this training could be obtained from:

- ❑ Postgraduate coursework
- ❑ Reliable and reputable training workshops and seminars provided by qualified presenters
- ❑ Specialized consultation with experts
- ❑ Membership and participation in professional associations and conferences that offer standard-specific training and development
- ❑ Other counseling-related training resources

For those who desire to become an AMHCA Clinical Mental Health Counseling Specialist, the skills outlined in this document can be measured, for example, through:

- ❑ Comprehension testing
- ❑ Elective procurement of certifications
- ❑ Verification of standard-specific attendance at training events
- ❑ Approval from insurance panels to meet their credentialing standards

A. Biological Bases of Behavior

The origins of human thought, feeling, and behavior, from the more to the less adaptive, are the result of complex interactions between biological, psychological, and social factors. There is an increased need for an expanded exploration and understanding of the biological factors as well as the way that they influence and are influenced by the psychological and social factors. A deeper understanding of the biological bases of behavior helps clinical mental health counselors not only be more precise in our diagnosis and treatment of mental disorders, but also in the promotion of wellness, peak performance, and quality of life.

1. **Knowledge**
    a. Understand the structure and function of the central nervous system (CNS) (brain, spinal cord) and the peripheral nervous system (PNS) (somatic, autonomic, sympathetic, and parasympathetic).

b. Understand how the human nervous system interacts with other physiological systems (endocrine, immune, gastrointestinal, etc.).

c. Possess a basic understanding of neural development across the life span (e.g., genetic, social, and/or environmental factors that influence the development of the human nervous system).

d. Comprehend structural and functional neuroanatomy as well as physiology of the sympathetic and parasympathetic nervous systems.

e. Understand physiological and biochemical mechanisms of intraneuronal communication (e.g., neurotransmission).

f. Comprehend methods used to evaluate functioning in the central and peripheral nervous systems (e.g., quantitative electroencephalography, MRI, galvanic skin response).

g. Possess an introductory knowledge of the neurocognitive processes underlying executive function, feelings, learning, memory, sensation, and perception across the life span.

h. Understand the neurobiological mechanisms underlying neurodevelopmental, neurodegenerative, and psychiatric disorders.

i. Comprehend the neurophysiological causes and behavioral implications of various medical conditions (e.g., autoimmune disorders, epilepsy, stroke, obesity) and traumatic brain injury.

j. Understand current research (e.g., mechanisms, efficacy, effectiveness) related to the use of biofeedback (e.g., neurofeedback, actigraphy data) for enhancing therapeutic outcomes in clinical mental health counseling.

k. Understand how drugs are absorbed, metabolized and eliminated.

l. Understand the pharmacokinetics and pharmacodynamics of psychotropic drugs used in the treatment of mental health disorders and neurodegenerative diseases.

m. Understand how psychotropic medications influence behavior change and is able to identify possible contraindications and adverse effects.

n. Understand the biological components of the therapeutic relationship.

2. **Skills**

    a. Integrating Research into Practice

        i. Acknowledge how science and evidence-based practice may be leveraged to improve outcomes and increase collaboration in integrated care settings.

        ii. Identify the limits of one's knowledge and professional expertise and regularly engage in ongoing continuing education and certification for additional specialty practice (e.g., biofeedback, neurofeedback).

        iii. Is able to locate, appraise, and assimilate research from allied fields such as neuroscience, endocrinology, immunology, nutrition, and psychiatry into clinical practice.

        iv. Critically evaluate peer-reviewed literature, communicates findings in a clear and accurate manner, and avoids overstating or overgeneralizing research findings.

        v. Demonstrate the ability to discuss the biology of reproduction and prenatal development with both clients and colleagues.

        vi. Describe the aging brain and how it may change across the life span.

vii. Explore the mechanisms and common clinical features of neurocognitive disorders in addition to offering strategies designed to improve functioning (e.g., agitation and anxiety, cognitive function, caregiver support) with clients, family and colleagues.

viii. Articulate how physiological (e.g., genes, molecules, circuits, immune functioning, endocrinology, gut microbiome), psychological (e.g., neurocognitive, personality, symptom), and environmental (e.g., individual, family, community, society, cultural) factors may interact to modulate human behavior.

ix. Articulate the basic principles of pharmacology (e.g., dose-response, side-effects, interactions pharmacokinetics, pharmacodynamics, routes of administration, distribution) and adaptation (e.g., tolerance, sensitization, withdrawal, placebo, nocebo) associated with commonly used drugs.

x. Review and critically appraise all research investigating the reliability and validity of any diagnostic and/or interventional technology intended to augment the practice of clinical mental health counseling, which may include emerging tools/methods used for collecting data from self-report or laboratory tests, mobile devices, and/ or other methods of physiological data collection (e.g., electroencephalography).

b. Clinical Intervention

i. Counsel clients from a biologically grounded life span developmental approach in concert with one's theoretical orientation.

ii. Acknowledge the strengths and limitations of drugs commonly used to treat major psychiatric disorders.

iii. Counsel clients about how to communicate with providers regarding the risks and benefits of medication, method of adherence, and common adverse effects.

iv. Effectively and accurately translate mental health information into plain language, without using scientific jargon, while also communicating empathy and ensuring a warm, non-judgmental, and supportive therapeutic alliance.

v. Render suitable diagnoses grounded in the synthesis of assessment data obtained from various methods (e.g., clinical interview, psychometric instruments, quantitative EEG) across multiple levels of explanation (e.g., genetic, molecular, cellular, neurocircuitry, physiology, behavior, and self-report).

vi. Produce timely, detailed, and accurate clinical reports which demonstrate: (1) the use of appropriate clinical terminology; (2) a commitment to ethical practice; (3) the ability to systematically collect and synthesize relevant data, and (4) how treatment is routinely refined and/or modified over time.

vii. Implement, at a minimum, formative and summative assessments to monitor progress and outcomes. viii. Effectively communicates and collaborates with medical and other allied health professionals.

viii. Use an appropriate biopsychosocial assessment to explore and enhance the quality of the therapeutic relationship.

c. Professional Advocacy

i. Consult with clients, the public, the media, and other professionals regarding the neurophysiological underpinnings of behavior and how the human nervous system adapts to life circumstances including traumatic brain injury, physical and sexual abuse and substance use.

ii. Remain up to date on emerging trends in mental health research (e.g., Research Domain Criteria) and practice (e.g., neurofeedback, precision psychiatry) so as to ensure that assessment, diagnosis, and interventions are continuously aligned to evidence-based treatments.

iii. Critically analyze emerging developments in mental health and social policy and engage in professional advocacy efforts to ensure that all clients have equitable access to ethical, sensitive, timely, and effective services.

iv. Partner with professional associations to offer ethical guidance and professional expertise to policy makers, the public, and colleagues from allied disciplines on emerging issues related to mental health policy.

B. Specialized Clinical Assessment

Licensed Clinical Mental Health Counselors (LCMHCs) are trained and qualified to conduct assessment and evaluation of clients' and their needs related to a plethora of dimensions in mental health functioning, not limited to the presence of symptoms and risk factors, mood, diagnostic measures for the purposes of treatment planning, intelligence, abilities, aptitude, personality, chemical dependence, impact of traumatic events on one's functioning, family structures and family dynamics, vocational and career development, and more. Graduate school standards and ongoing specific training and development prepare counselors to assess, diagnose, and provide feedback, form treatment planning goals, and anticipate future challenges or improvements. The range of assessment measures that LCMHCs utilize in clinical care are quite numerous, not limited to mental status examinations in the clinical session, clinical symptom checklists, non-structured and structured clinical interviews and observations, authenticated published assessment tools, understanding self-report, and qualitative measures.

This introduction to the standard on assessment and evaluation emphasizes three important considerations that LCMHCs should be mindful of when preparing, selecting, administering and interpreting or reporting test results. The first is a reminder to LCMHCs to be familiar with laws and ethics, with one's state of licensure, its laws and any stated limits that licensure codes assert related to the type of assessment that is legally permitted in the state within which one is licensed. State regulations, codes, and laws may evolve and change at a rate that is not synchronized with the routine updates to the *AMHCA Standards,* and so LCMHCs will want to remain informed and updated on one's legislative or licensure standards. Concomitantly, laws co-exist with a profession's codes of ethics, and LCMHCs are reminded to be fluent with the *AMHCA Code of Ethics* and its guidance on assessment and evaluation.

Secondly, as with all clinical care provided to consumers, related to all AMHCA standards, LCMHCs are urged to remain culturally sensitive in the process of selecting, administering and interpreting assessments with clients who may be members of minority groups. LCMHCs will select tests that have been normed on populations similar to the client, and consider cultural issues when interpreting assessment including primary language of the client, the use of translators, cultural bias of the test questions, and differences in performance on standardized tests among different racial/ethnic groups and by gender. Research and development of culturally sensitive assessments has been improving in recent years. However, LCMHCs are urged to remain at the forefront of best practices in assessment that respect and strive for maximal inclusivity and sensitivity to the cultural traits of diverse populations.

Finally, LCMHCs should be aware that training and scope of competence is not limited to graduate school training. For the myriad of assessment measures available on the market to assess traits important to clients' functioning, each publisher of any given measure may recommend or require its own criteria for training, certification, or approval as a competent administrator of said assessment.

Appendix B: AMHCA Standards for the Practice of Clinical Mental Health Counseling

Some publishers may require credentials above the baseline of a graduate degree in counseling and may require training or ongoing renewal of certifications to maintain proficiency with the use of specialized assessments.

LCMHCs are encouraged to consult with AMHCA's collaborators, that is, a joint statement of *Standards for Assessment in Mental Health Counseling* that was developed collaboratively with the former Association for Assessment in Counseling and Education (AACE) and AMHCA. AACE is now the Association for Assessment and Research in Counseling (AARC). In addition to consulting this statement for updating and revising the Specialized Clinical Assessment standard, the ACPC also referred to two other position papers. The *CACREP Standards* (2016) provided a reminder of the baseline assessment and evaluation skills that counselors are trained in, and also the committee consulted an analysis by the National Board of Forensic Evaluators, *Can Licensed Mental Health Counselors Administer and Interpret Psychological Tests?* (2018). The ACPC referred to these position papers in the development of this version of the standard and gratefully acknowledge their contributions.

Clinical mental health counselors may administer and interpret psychological tests provided they receive appropriate training, which shall include the following:

1. **Knowledge**

    a. Examine the nature, meaning and purpose of assessment in counseling (including historical perspectives).

    b. Differentiate between methods of preparing for and conducting initial assessments.

    c. Understand the use of assessments for diagnostic and treatment planning purposes with developmental, behavioral, and mental disorders.

    d. Distinguish basic concepts of standardized and non-standardized testing, and other assessment techniques (e.g., norm-referenced and criterion-referenced assessments, structured and semi-structured, and qualitative procedures, etc.).

    e. Interpret and apply statistical concepts (e.g., scales of measurement, measures of central tendency, indices of variability, shapes and types of distributions, and correlations, etc.).

    f. Interpret the concept of reliability as it applies to the use in assessments (i.e., theory of measurement error, models of reliability, and the use of reliability information).

    g. Interpret the concept of validity as it applies to the use in assessments (i.e., evidence of validity, types of validity, and the relationship between reliability and validity).

    h. Understand the use of assessments relevant to personal/social development, environmental/behavioral, and personality/psychological testing.

    i. Distinguish factors related to the assessment and evaluation of individuals, groups, and specific populations (e.g., aggression, suicide, trauma, individuals from diverse backgrounds, etc.).

    j. Differentiate between ethical strategies for selecting, administering, and interpreting assessment and evaluation of test results.

    k. Understand the intent, purpose, scoring/analysis and interpretive expectations for each utilized assessment (as defined in the assessment manual/protocol).

2. **Skills**

   a. Apply effective methods to select, administer, score, analyze and interpret assessment results.

   b. Select, administer, analyze and interpret test results with special attention to cultural traits of the clients, using primary language of the client appropriate use of translators, any cultural bias of test questions, differences in performance on standardized tests among different racial or ethnic group or by gender.

   c. Critically evaluate assessments, identifying basic statistical concepts (such as types and acceptable levels of reliability and validity, norming methods, etc.) and obtaining instruments for mental health counseling and special populations (e.g., visually impaired, intellectual disability, mental health disability, etc.).

   d. Demonstrate the ability to effectively prepare for and conduct initial assessment meetings.

   e. Employ a broad spectrum of assessments, including personal/social development, environmental/behavioral, and personality/psychological instruments.

   f. Utilize assessment results to develop effective treatment plan goals, objectives and interventions.

   g. Provide quality client care in the explanation of assessment, informed consent and communication of results.

   h. Demonstrate the ability to identify the appropriate use for assessments (e.g., the intended use of the test, promotion of greater mental health and in a manner that will cause no harm to the participant).

   i. Understand the use of assessments for diagnostic and treatment planning purposes with developmental, behavioral, and mental disorders.

   j. Understand the use of assessments relevant to personal/social development, environmental/behavioral, personality/psychological testing.

   k. Distinguish factors related to the assessment and evaluation of individuals, groups, and specific populations (e.g., aggression, suicide, trauma, etc.).

C. Trauma-Informed Care

Many individuals seek counseling to resolve symptoms associated with traumatic or chronically distressful experiences. Those experiences may include single-episode traumatic events (such as a mugging, assault, tornado, etc.), or complex trauma (sometimes referred to as developmental trauma or poly-victimization) experienced in childhood, adolescence, or adulthood featuring chronic abuse, neglect, or exposure to other harsh adversities.

The types of traumatic or persistently distressful experiences that can result in symptoms and disorders are many. As more is learned about the causes of trauma-related symptoms, the nomenclature within a trauma-informed care approach has grown, and the descriptors for trauma are numerous. Some examples in this non-exhaustive list that are based on existing literature, research, models and methods might include betrayal trauma, domestic trauma, forced displacement trauma, historical trauma, military trauma, moral trauma, polytrauma, system induced trauma and re-traumatization, refugee and/or war zone trauma, medical trauma, toxic stress, and more. For the purposes of this standard, the terms trauma, chronic distress, toxic stress, and/or complex trauma will be used to encompass the meaning of all types and causes of trauma.

LCMHCs obtain knowledge and skills to treat clients who experience(d) traumatic events or conditions, chronic distress, and complex trauma; this preparation is essential for the practice of clinical mental health due to the high incidence of trauma and distressful events or contexts. Individuals who have the symptoms of unresolved complex trauma, chronic distress, or other traumas are at risk for a variety of emotional, cognitive, and physical illnesses that can potentially last throughout their lives. Therefore, these individuals frequently present with related co-occurring disorders, such as anxiety, depression, and substance use, and often form negative core self-beliefs. Recent research reveals that physical health later in one's life span may be compromised due to trauma. The presence of resilience is an important mitigating variable in the progression of symptoms related to traumatic experiences. Complex trauma can often compromise an individual's resilience or capacity to thrive after traumatic experiences compared to persons who survived a single-episode traumatic event such as a car accident.

It is important to note that the traumatic event is a cause of the related disorders or symptoms as contrasted with unwittingly regarding the client as the cause of the symptoms. Though the aftereffects of traumatic experiences can be very profound and experienced internally within traumatized individuals, the cause of the trauma is almost always related to external events, actions, or contexts that are outside of the individual. LCMHCs also want to note if the cause(s) of the trauma are natural (e.g., a tornado or hurricane) or human caused (e.g., domestic violence, maltreatment, terrorism). Human-caused traumas frequently create more vexing emotional repercussions. Additionally, clinicians should remain well-informed about neurological effects of chronic distress or exposure to repeated traumatic experiences which compromise a person's ability to develop effective coping measures.

All competent clinical mental health counselors possess the knowledge and skills necessary to offer trauma assessment, diagnosis, and effective treatment while utilizing techniques that emerge from evidence-based practices and best practices.

1. **Knowledge**
   a. Recognize that the type and context of trauma has important implications for the etiology, sequelae of symptoms, diagnosis, and treatment of symptoms (e.g., ongoing sexual abuse in childhood is qualitatively different from war trauma for young adult soldiers).
   b. Know how trauma-causing events may impact individuals differently in relation to social context, prior history of traumatic experiences, age, gender, sexual orientation, developmental level, culture, ethnicity, access to care, resilience, etc.
   c. Understand that symptoms faced as a result of traumatic experiences can be multifaceted and therefore LCMHCs should be familiar with its many forms including relational, acute, chronic, episodic, and complex, as well as the implications for effective, evidenced-based treatment approaches.
   d. Recognize the circumstances or indicators when a referral to a more qualified mental health professional who specializes in trauma is warranted. Indications that a more trauma-focused approach is needed may be related to severity, complexity, responsiveness of the client to lower-level of care, capacity of the LCMHC to provide specialized care, etc. More specialized care may be found in services such as inpatient care, trauma intensive-care, Eye Movement Desensitization Reprocessing, Trauma-Focused CBT, and other recognized evidence-based approaches.
   e. Understand the impact of various types of trauma (e.g., sexual and physical abuse, war, chronic verbal/emotional abuse, neglect, natural disasters, etc.) may have on the Central Nervous System (CNS) and the Autonomic Nervous System (ANS) and how this might impact one's sense of secure attachment, affect regulation, personality functioning, self-

beliefs and self-identity, self-care, etc., as well as the potential for trauma-related re-enactment in relationships.

    f. Recognize the long-term consequences of trauma-causing events on social groups, communities, and cultures, including the incidence of collective trauma, generationally-transmitted and "historical" trauma. LCMHCs may serve communities and assist with the impact of collective trauma in a variety of formats or settings, such as with families, agencies and organizations, municipalities, multisystemic collaborations, etc., through various modalities such as psychoeducation, consultation, information provision with the media, follow-up initiatives, preventative initiatives, etc.

    g. Understand how promoting and developing resiliency and other protective factors for individuals, groups, and communities can diminish the risk and impact of trauma related disorders.

    h. Recognize differential strategies and approaches necessary to work with children, adolescents, adults, couples, and families in trauma treatment.

    i. Recognize, from an organizational or management perspective, the need to design, train, and implement trauma-informed care policies and practices for a systemically responsive approach to serving clients impacted by traumatic experiences (e.g., train the Security Guards who work in a domestic violence shelter how to carry out their duties with trauma-informed awareness).

    j. Understand familiarity with trauma stewardship and effective practices for self-care, as well as strategies to protect from secondary or vicarious traumatization.

    k. Understand the indicators or target outcomes of effective and enduring trauma resolution (e.g., the integration of traumatic memory into the client's regular memory, traumatic event recall without debilitating emotional distress, individual generalized affect regulation, the alleviation of traumatic triggers, post-traumatic growth, etc.).

    l. Understand the well-timed exploration of the potential for and themes for post-traumatic growth (PTG) among traumatized clients after effective counseling and symptom reduction. LCMHCs may assist clients to discover ways in which a survivor may change for the positive (e.g., changes in one's sense of priorities, a greater appreciation of life, a deepened sense of personal strength, more meaningful relationships, a sense of new possibilities for oneself, developing views and philosophy about life, and/or the meaning of suffering, perspective, or a strengthened belief system).

2. **Skills**

    a. Demonstrate the ability to use evidence-based assessment measures to evaluate and differentiate the clinical impact of various trauma-causing events, not limited to evaluation measures/resources focused on early life trauma and distress, such as the Adverse Childhood Experiences Survey, along with the many other trauma assessment tools available for type-of-trauma measures throughout the life span.

    b. Demonstrate the ability to apply established counseling theories that are evidence-based or best trauma resolution practices. Best practices promote the integration of brain functioning and resolution of cognitive, emotional, sensory, and behavioral symptoms related to trauma-causing events for socially and culturally diverse clients across the life span.

    c. Demonstrate sensitivity to individual and psychosocial factors that interact with trauma-causing events in counseling and treatment planning.

d. Demonstrate familiarity with trauma stewardship and effective practices for self-care, and for protection from secondary or vicarious traumatization.

e. Demonstrate the ability to recognize that any of the clinical mental health counselor's traumatic experiences may impact his or her trauma-surviving-clients and the counseling process. LCMHCs should seek appropriate trauma resolution counseling and/or consultation as necessary.

f. Apply age-appropriate strategies and approaches in assessing and counseling children and adolescents and modify these techniques when working with adults.

g. Use differentially appropriate counseling and other treatment interventions in the treatment of couples who encounter re-enactment trauma, trauma of a partner, or secondary trauma from traumatized family members.

h. Demonstrate the ability to advocate with payors of counseling fees (e.g., insurance companies, treatment centers, etc.) by monitoring diagnosis and treatment needs with utilization review of sessions allotment. Clinicians may have to advocate rigorously for the client with the payor of counseling fees and itemize thoroughly all diagnosed comorbid disorders while also assuring the client about the differences of "what's wrong with me" vs. "what happened to me."

i. Demonstrate how to comprehensively assess the degree of trauma resolution as a measure of client recovery as well as an indicator of therapeutic efficacy. LCMHCs should monitor ongoing clinical progress toward target outcomes, using assessment measures, and client self-report to ensure that mutual counselor/client termination of care (contrasted with premature cessation of counseling by either party) yields healthy and positive outcomes.

j. Demonstrate the ability to facilitate the development of clients' sense of safety and resilience.

k. Provide assessment and guidance with a traumatized client related to post-traumatic growth (PTG) in a clinically time sensitive manner (after symptom reduction) to explore possible avenues for the client to discover personal changes or qualities within oneself, in relationships, or in belief systems and meaning-making that may have emerged from the traumatic experience(s) and its impact on self.

D. Substance Use Disorders and Co-occurring Disorders

Substance use disorders (SUDs) are commonly comorbid with other mental health disorders. In other words, individuals with substance use often have a mental health condition concurrently. For example, having Post-Traumatic Stress Disorder (PTSD) is frequently a significant contributing factor to the development of a substance use disorder. Many experts acknowledge that one mental health diagnosis can result in a substance use disorder, and also, it is possible for a substance use disorder to cause mental health disorders or other illnesses. Failure to address both the mental health disorder or other illnesses as well as the substance-related disorder can result in ineffective and incomplete treatment, stabilization, or recovery.

There can be are many consequences of undiagnosed, untreated, or undertreated comorbid disorders including a higher potential for homelessness, incarceration, medical illnesses, suicide, danger to others, and premature death, to name a few. It is incumbent on LCMHCs to apply thorough and comprehensive assessment and treatment for co-occurring disorders to prevent such neglect, harm, and possible death. The knowledge and skills recommendations below are a guide to effective practice when working with clients affected by SUDs and co-occurring disorders.

1. **Knowledge**
    a. Understand the epidemiology (incidence, distribution, and control) of substance use and co-occurring disorders for socially and culturally diverse populations at risk across the life span.
    b. Understand theories and models about the etiology of substance use and co-occurring disorders including risk and resiliency factors for individuals, groups, and communities. Explanations for the development of SUDs are multiple, including:
        i. Psychological Models (behavioral, learning, cognitive, psychoanalytic, personality, social learning)
        ii. Multi-Causal Models (biopsychosocial, syndrome, integral)
        iii. Biological/Physiological Models (disease, genetic predisposition, co-occurring)
        iv. Educational/Knowledge Models (educational, public health, developmental)
        v. Psychosocial Model (peer-cluster, problem behavior)
        vi. Sociocultural Models (sociocultural, culture-specific, prescriptive, sanctioned-use)
        vii. Family Models (general systems, parental influence)
        viii. Lifestyle/Coping Models (stress-coping, lifestyle, spiritual)
        ix. Progression Models (gateway, final common pathway)
        x. Choice/Moral Models

    Additionally, LCMHCs should become familiar with "abstinence-focused" and "harm reduction-focused" views of and approaches for understanding and treating substance use.

    c. Possess a working knowledge of the neurological and biological aspects of SUDs, both related to the causes and treatment implications for SUDs.
    d. Possess a working knowledge of SUDs including drug types, routes of administration, drug distribution, elimination, dependence, tolerance, withdrawal, dose response interaction, and how to interpret basic lab results.
    e. Recognize the capacity for substance use to present as one of a range of psychological or medical disorders, to cause such disorders, and understand effective assessment and differential diagnosis among SUDs and other diagnoses.
    f. Understand treatment and clinical management of SUDs with the presence of co-occurring mental health disorders with an emphasis on best practices, risk management and prioritization of clinical goals, medication management, and theory/method/ approach match for each condition (such as cognitive behavioral, trauma-focused, dialectical behavioral, etc.).
    g. Possess a working knowledge of how prevention, treatment, aftercare, and recovery policies and programs function.
    h. Understand the working definition of recovery and recovery oriented systems of care for mental illness and SUDs with familiarity and promotion of recovery support strategic initiatives that focus on health (physical and emotional well-being), home (stable, safe living arrangements), purpose (meaningful daily activities to participate in society), and community (social relationships involving support, friendship, love and hope).
    i. Possess a working knowledge of the ten guiding principles for recovery from mental illness and SUDs (hope, person driven, many pathways, holistic, peer support, relational, culturally based, addresses trauma, strengths and responsibility, and respect).

j. Possess a working knowledge of recovery support tools and resources that include peer support programs or models that demonstrate peer-navigators' competencies, decision-making tools, use of narratives and stories, parents and families, communities and social resources, and other training tools.

k. Study the rapidly developing facts and emerging community and clinical responses related to the widespread abuse of opioid and other prescription drugs, along with initiatives and response strategies, such as the evidenced-based publications from researchers, experts, foundations, and advocacy groups.

l. Understand which medications and psychopharmacological treatments may be effective for the treatment of alcohol use disorder, and abuse of opioid and other prescription drugs, as well as pharmacological treatments of other co-morbid conditions (such as mood and anxiety disorders, etc.).

m. Understand the current history, philosophy, and trends in substance use counseling, including treatments that incorporate:
   i. Stages of change
   ii. Motivational interviewing
   iii. Self-help, spiritual, and secular groups and communities (not limited to 12-step groups, Self-Management and Recovery Training [SMART], Secular Organizations for Sobriety [SOS], Refuge Recovery, Life Ring Secular Recovery, Moderation Management, Celebrate Recovery, etc.)
   iv. Medication-assisted treatment in conjunction with clinical mental health counseling

n. Understand the application of existing therapeutic approaches and counseling techniques empirically-validated for addictions counseling, such as Motivational Interviewing, Cognitive Behavioral, Contingency Management, Motivational Enhancement Therapy, Life Skills Training, Acceptance and Commitment Therapy, Dialectical Behavioral Therapy, Functional Analytic Therapy, Mindfulness Based Cognitive Behavioral Therapy, etc.

o. Understand ethical and legal implications related to counseling practice for substance use disorders and cooccurring disorders in diverse settings, particularly, including familiarity with the co-occurrence of legal problems with SUDs. LCMHCs should be familiar with addiction-oriented treatment options for legal difficulties, inpatient or outpatient units, partial or day programs, recovery houses or sober living communities. LCMHCs are advised to be aware of criminal justice system options, with attention to community "mental health courts" or "drug courts" that encourage alternative sentencing as a treatment strategy in lieu of incarceration and should be familiar with Title 42 Code of Federal Regulations (42 CFR) when working with individuals who have protection under this code.

2. **Skills**

a. Demonstrate the ability to effectively assess and screen for unhealthy substance use such as but not limited to alcohol, marijuana, tobacco, and other licit and illicit drugs, that relies on validated screening and assessment procedures, including recommendations for placement criteria.

b. Demonstrate the ability to gauge the severity of clients' cooccurring disorders and to assess their stage of readiness for change.

c. Demonstrate the ability to provide brief interventions and counseling, care management, for unhealthy alcohol, tobacco, prescription drug and opioid use disorders.

d. Conceptualize cases and develop treatment plans based on stages of change that address mental health and substance use disorders simultaneously.

e. Demonstrate skills in applying motivational enhancement strategies to engage clients.

f. Provide appropriate counseling strategies when working with clients who have co-occurring disorders while first prioritizing symptom reduction or symptom management in order of most dangerous (if left untreated) to client or others.

g. Demonstrate the ability to provide counseling and education about substance use disorders, and mental/emotional disorders to families and others who are affected by clients with cooccurring disorders, including incorporating systemically oriented family counseling into treatment planning and/or providing appropriate referrals.

h. Demonstrate the ability to modify counseling systems, theories, techniques, and interventions for socially and culturally diverse clients with co-occurring disorders across the life span that are consistent with evidence-based best practices.

i. Demonstrate the ability to recognize one's own limitations when treating co-occurring disorders and to seek collaboration, consultation, training, supervision appropriately, and/or one's own therapy, or refer clients as needed.

j. Demonstrate the ability to apply and adhere to ethical and legal standards in substance use disorders and co-occurring disorder counseling. This includes competence related to assisting clients who navigate the legal implications of SUDs and systems such as drug courts, mental health courts, legal case management, court-recommended treatment, incarceration and sentencing trends, 42 CFR, etc.

k. Broaden counseling and therapy skills to provide multiple modalities of counseling-related functions not limited to psychoeducation and client education, case management, multisystem collaboration (for example, with "Drug Courts," housing, women and infant care resources, group counseling and support group provisioning, sober living and independent living resourcing, etc.).

E. Technology Supported Counseling and Communications (TSCC)

Technology supported counseling and communications (TSCC) has been described as tele-mental health or telehealth, e-health, telecare, distance counseling, virtual counseling, etc. It is an intentionally broad term referring to the provision of mental health services from a distance to clients through the use of technology. TSCC occurs when the counselor and the client are in two different physical locations. TSCC also refers to the use of technology to support the administration or non-clinical management of counseling services, often related to communications, practice/agency software and portals, and social media.

The mental health profession is swiftly adapting to the use of advanced communication technologies for not only the delivery of care and mental health services, but also for supporting the provision of services administratively such as making or confirming appointments, record-keeping, billing and collecting fees, etc. By using advanced communication technologies, Licensed Clinical Mental Health Counselors (LCMHCs) are able to widen their reach to clients in a cost-effective manner, making available services to clients in many geographic areas, ameliorating the mal-distribution of general and specialty care, while increasing services for persons who otherwise might have found counseling to have been inaccessible for a variety of reasons. The establishment of clear TSCC guidelines for counselors and clients improves clinical outcomes while promoting informed consent and reasonable client expectations.

This section provides guidance on clinical, technical, administrative and ethical issues related to electronic counseling and communication between LCMHCs and clients using advances in TSCC. Counseling may be provided synchronously via audio/video or virtual conferencing, by voice telephonically, or with synchronous chat, text, or SMS medium, or asynchronously through email. Communications used to support the provision of counseling services may include counseling practice software, portals, and data management options for record-keeping including but not limited to "cloud" storage options, appointment management, and the billing and collecting of fees.

The standard emphasizes two of the more important dynamics related to technology supported counseling and communications: 1) safety, risk prevention, and risk management for clients who may be more vulnerable when receiving counseling via technology, and 2) protection of identity and confidentiality. These guidelines also serve as a companion to *AMHCA's Code of Ethics*, specifically its section on Technology Supported Counseling and Communications.

Additionally, since each state may have variable laws and regulations related to technology and mental health service delivery, LCMHCs are urged to be familiar with the legal guidance in their respective states and plan to provide counseling to clients who have residence where the LCMHC is licensed. For example, state regulations have varying rules related to whether or not the LCMHC or the client has to be in the same state geographically simultaneously at the time of the service, whereas other states may allow bi-state or two locations as long as the client is a resident of the state or territory wherein the LCMHC is credentialed.

The following will review Knowledge and Skill digital competencies for both the counseling functions and the communications functions.

As a final note, AMHCA's Advancement for Clinical Practice Committee has asserted the need and expectation that this particular standard will be reviewed and updated more frequently than other standards that come up for review on a regular rotation, due to the rapid emergence of knowledge, software, application, products, and best practices related to technology supported counseling and communication.

1. **Knowledge**
    a. Counseling
        i. Recognize that training and certification are recommended prerequisites to provide ethical and clinical counseling services using technology. LCMHCs should familiarize themselves with the training and certification options. They should prepare to obtain and update valid proficiency to provide TSCC. Fifteen hours of course instruction is recommended as a minimum.
        ii. Possess a strong working knowledge of TSCC, which includes:
            a) Synchronous modalities (telephone, audio/videoconferencing [or virtual conferencing], text/chat/SMS-based)
            b) Non-synchronous modalities (e-mail)
        iii. Prior to providing services to a client, understand the elements involved in conducting a fitness-for-technology-supported counseling risk assessment.
        iv. Know how to partner with counseling resources near the client.
        v. Know that, whenever possible, LCMHCs will meet in a face-to-face session to assess client needs prior to utilizing TSCC. Whether a first appointment is face-to-face or technologically supported, a fitness-for-technology-supported counseling risk assessment will still be conducted prior to providing mental health counseling.

vi. Demonstrate understanding of best practices of service delivery described in the empirical literature and professional standards—including multicultural considerations—relevant to the TSCC service modality being offered not limited to the clients' technological and other abilities to engage in TSCC, communication mores and technology-specific language use, along with abilities or symptoms that may preclude or impede face-to-face counseling services.

vii. Understand all aspects of informed consent and the procurement of prospective and current clients' informed consent related to the risks and benefits of TSCC, the collaborative selection process of choosing a modality, and agreement between client and TSCC counselor about how the technology will be used or not used in the provision of services.

viii. Recognize the need to communicate clearly and to obtain written informed consent for all TSCC modalities utilized, understand how to adhere to all ethical and legal guidelines for counseling (especially those germane not only to the profession but also to one's respective state laws and codes), and provide informed consent related to confidentiality specifically with TSCC, encryption, availability, determination of emergency intervention measures if needed, etc.

ix. Understand that TSCC is changing rapidly and anticipate that new modalities of communication with clients will continuously emerge and require clinical, ethical and legal guidance and/or training and even possibly renewed certification.

x. Understand and comply with one's respective state laws governing or relating to TSCC which may include the following considerations:

xi. Understand and recognize scope of practice and jurisdiction matters related to many state laws which commonly require that mental health professionals be licensed in the state in which a client is receiving or residing counseling.

xii. LCMHCs who regularly provide mental health counseling across state borders should be fully compliant with all applicable state laws where the client resides and have prior approval from the client's state's board of examiners in counseling to provide said services. Prior familiarity with other states geographic rules is essential, for example, to determine if regulations expect that both the client and the LCMHC be in the same state simultaneously with the provision of the service.

xiii. Become knowledgeable with protocols when circumstances may require special ethical and clinical consideration be afforded to clients in unique situations for short term counseling service and continuity of care. In the event that clients who generally reside in a state where the LCMHC is licensed, but who will be away from their residence, LCMHCs will assure continuity of care while also seeking provisions to either refer or obtain permission from a distant state's or country's regulatory body in examples when:

   a) Individuals who temporarily travel out of their state for business, personal, or other purposes need to receive services from their LCMHCs.

   b) Individuals who relocate to another state who require continuing care until they have obtained the services of a new LCMHC/mental health professional if the current practitioner is not licensed in the client's new state of residence.

   c) Individuals who are relocating to another country where psychotherapy services may not be available, and who may warrant continuing treatment.

d) Familiarity with the "other" state's or country's provisions for a "grace period" and for how long that period permits service provision or if the state issues a longer-term distance counseling license expressly for that LCMHC and client to work together.

xiv. LCMHCs will provide timely and ample informed consent to clients who change residences or locations about the need for referral if distance counseling is not possible with the existing credentials of or authorizations extended to the LCMHC.

xv. Stay up to date with relevant changes to laws and continuously consult with ethical and legal experts about ongoing developments and trends in the confidential, safe, and therapeutic dynamics related to distance counseling.

xvi. Have a working knowledge of how TSCC adheres to policies within the Americans With Disabilities Act (ADA). LCMHCs will seek ways to make appropriate accommodations, provided that the client or prospective client is not in risk and is assessed for "fitness for distance counseling."

xvii. Know that provisions for emergency intervention will include, as a priority when possible, face-to-face counseling or the provision of a geographically accessible (to the client) LCMHC or other mental health provider, with the inclusion of the TSCC counselor as part of a comprehensive care management plan. The TSCC-LCMHC will have identified and established geographically nearby (to the client) emergency response resources such as known agencies and options prior to beginning counseling if there arises an emergency or threat of harm or danger to self of others. Some examples (non-exhaustive here) may include direct 9-1-1 phone lines in specific localities, fire and first responder agencies, emergency rooms and hospitals, domestic violence shelters, and local crisis response services. The LCMHC will have established, prior to beginning counseling, the client's safe therapy partner with contact information so that the partner can be engaged in emergency situations with immediacy.

xviii. Recognize that synchronous or live communication counseling modalities compared to non-synchronous communication are generally easier to monitor a client's safety and therefore is recommended or preferred in the interest of quality assurance and safety of the client when crisis or emergent situations seem imminent, are unfolding or require active intervention.

xix. Recognize the importance of retaining records and copies of all correspondence in regard to text-based communications and related electronic information (including emails, text messages, written correspondence, etc.) in a manner that protects privacy and meets the standards of HIPAA regulations and the Health Information Technology for Economic and Clinical Health Act (HITECH Act).

xx. Know that confidential and privileged communications using text-based communication TSCC should be encrypted securely whenever possible.

b. Communications

i. Understand the importance of maintaining boundaries in the use of social media which should be continuously monitored and updated, including privacy settings in all social media. LCMHCs should differentiate personal and professional forms of social media and keep these separate, including maintaining personal account names that are unlikely to be identified or known by clients.

ii. All informed consent materials along with disclaimers on the LCMHC's social media, such as but not limited to Facebook, Twitter, Instagram, Linked In, etc., will clarify exactly how a client will appropriately and securely contact the LCMHC in ways other than through social media, and also explain that social media is not a means through which personal information can be or will be shared. Further, the LCMHC does not provide direct care and response through social media and clients should be instructed clearly in both informed consent forms and prominently on social media sites to not rely or expect this.

    iii. LCMHCs will refrain from searching for or obtaining information about clients via the clients' identities in the internet and will not search or study clients' narratives via any social media options, unless the client has specifically directed the LCMHC to do so for a specific therapeutic purpose with proper documentation, and within a certain timeline.

    iv. LCMHCs will understand that they should not solicit from clients their feedback for social media sites or other published media in order to promote or authenticate the LCMHC's performance or services. Additionally, clients should be pre-informed that if the client offers feedback about their LCMHC, there will be no response from the LCMHC, and that confidentiality may be compromised if the client posts such feedback.

2. Skills

  a. General

    i. Demonstrate proficiency with technological modalities being used such as synchronous modalities (e.g., video-conferencing or virtual conferencing) and non-synchronous modalities (e.g., texting, emailing).

    ii. Demonstrate digital competence and the ability to anticipate and adapt to emerging technologies and adopt those techniques to address the needs of clients to enhance quality of care to them. Conversely, the LCMHC will discuss appropriate options for the client if or when TSCC becomes counter-therapeutic.

    iii. Possess the ability to carefully examine and to assess for the unique benefits of delivering TSCC services (e.g., access to care, adaptive technology for differing abilities, etc.) relative to the unique risks (e.g., safety of client, information security, therapeutic alliance, etc.) when determining whether or not to offer TSCC services.

    iv. Continually communicate any risks and benefits of the TSCC services to the client, and document such communication, preferably during in-person contact with the client, and facilitate an active discussion on these issues when conducting screening for fitness for distance counseling, intake, and initial assessment.

  b. Assessment

    i. Demonstrate digital competence in assessing the appropriateness of the TSCC services to be provided for the client. Assessment may include:

      a) The examination of the potential risks and benefits of TSCC services for clients' particular needs;

      b) A review of the most appropriate medium (e.g., video teleconference, text, email, etc.);

      c) The client's situation/locality within the home or within an organizational context;

    ii. Prepare for service delivery options (for example, if in-person services are ever available);

Appendix B: *AMHCA Standards for the Practice of Clinical Mental Health Counseling*

- a) The availability of geographically near crisis or emergency, or technical personnel or supports;
- b) The multicultural, ability level, legal, clinical and ethical issues that may impact the client's safety or therapeutic conditions;
- c) Risk of distractions or possible technological limitations or failures in session related to reception, connectivity, band width, streaming, power sources, etc.;
- d) Potential for privacy breaches and subsequent protective measures; and
- e) Other impediments that may impact the effective delivery of TSCC services.

  iii. Demonstrate the ability to monitor and engage in the continual assessment of the client's progress when offering TSCC services to determine if the provision of services is appropriate and beneficial to the client while anticipating and providing other therapeutic supports if needed.

c. Emergency Considerations:

  i. Demonstrate reasonable efforts, at the onset of service, to identify and learn how to access relevant and appropriate emergency resources in the client's local area. These should include:

  - a) Emergency response contacts,
  - b) Emergency telephone numbers,
  - c) Hospital admissions and/or emergency department,
  - d) Local referral resources,
  - e) Client-safety advocate (clinical champion) at a partner clinic where services are delivered, and
  - f) Other support individuals such as a trusted family member, friend, or ally in the client's life when available.

  ii. Establish clear and specific instructions that is provided to all clients for what to do in an emergency.

d. Multicultural Considerations

  i. Demonstrate an understanding of specific issues that may arise with diverse populations that could impact assessment when providing or considering TSCC. LCMHCs should make appropriate arrangements to address those concerns including but not limited to language or cultural issues; cognitive, physical or sensory skills or impairments; transportation needs; rural resident needs; elderly considerations and needs for appropriate adaptive technology.

e. Special Needs

  i. Demonstrate reasonable skill in accepting and addressing special needs of clients in adhering to appropriate ADA provisions.

  ii. Make appropriate arrangements for individuals with differing abilities to accommodate special needs, for example, such related to sight and hearing impairments.

f. Communications

  i. LCMHCs should explore and install all available technologically advanced features for telephone, computer, and devices such as laptop and tablet services that ensure encryption and which safeguard the identity and confidentiality of a clients' communications and records with the LCMHC for both counseling and general administrative communications (e.g., setting up appointments, billing and collecting fees, etc.). These features may include practice management software, documentation of sessions, billing, appointment management, texting, or emailing communication, etc.

    ii. The Social Media Policy will contain clearly stated instructions for the LCMHC's preferred methods of contact, including:

        a) LCMHCs will instruct clients that the LCMHC's professional social media sites will not be a venue for direct contact, and that clients' posts may be a breach of their confidentiality.

        b) LCMHCs will maintain their own personal social media with identity and monikers distinctly different from their professional social media sites.

    iii. LCMHCs will develop a Social Media Policy (SMP) that will be included with, shared, explained, and updated in the informed consent process. Some elements of the SMP should include but may not be limited to the following:

        a) *Friending:* The LCMHC addresses the concept of "friending" and explains that they will not be able to accept friend requests or issue friend requests via social media apps.

        b) *Liking or Following:* Similarly, the SMP defines clients' "Liking" or "Following" and that they present threats to the client's confidentiality, while also explaining that the LCMHC may delete clients' posts at their discretion.

        c) *Texting or Messaging:* The LCMHC will use encrypted texting apps if texting is formally considered to be a way for the client and clinician to communicate.

        d) *Emails:* Emailing will be done only with encrypted protection, and if it is a formally accepted and stated way to communicate. Otherwise, emails will be limited and used with discretion.

        e) *Search Engines:* Using search engines and researching clients' online thumbprint or identity will be prohibited unless at the specific and documented request of the client for a specific therapeutic reason and duration.

        f) *Business Site Reviews:* Clarify the implications if the client uses business review sites to rank or provide feedback about the LCMHC and their services, that the LCMHC may not see this feedback, and will not be able to provide a response to it outside of the counseling session. The LCMHC will refrain from requesting clients to provide reviews.

        g) *Location-Based Services:* Encourage the client to disable Location-Based Services (LBS) which may signal to the client's social media followers that they are visiting a counseling agency address.

    iv. Emphasize that LCMHCs will refrain from using social media to conduct counseling or communications with clients and instruct clients clearly that social media cannot be a way to get in contact with the LCMHC.

F. Integrated Behavioral Health Care Counseling

The integration of clinical mental health counseling with primary care and other medical services is required to achieve better patient health outcomes. Integrated systems of medical and behavioral care

are comprehensive, coordinated, multidisciplinary, and co-located through the latest technologies. Clinical mental health counselors must continually increase their knowledge and skills to participate in these emerging practices and systems through the use of evidence-based treatment approaches. In order to stress the vital importance of integrated behavioral health counseling, please see the AMHCA white paper entitled Behavioral Health Counseling in Health Care Integration Practices and Health Care Systems.

Integrated health care is the systematic coordination of behavioral health care with primary care medical services. Episodic and point-of-service treatment which has not included behavioral health care has proven to be ineffective, inefficient, and costly for chronic behavioral and medical illnesses. By contrast, the integrated behavioral health care assessment and treatment of patient psychiatric disorders strongly correlates with positive medical health outcomes. For example, many gastro-intestinal health outcomes rely on the effective treatment of anxiety disorders. By employing all-inclusive behavioral health interventions, skilled LCMHCs assist patients to realize optimal human functioning as they alleviate emotional and mental distress.

LCMHCs have the ethical responsibility to possess the training and experience to promote health from their unique perspective of prevention, wellness, and personal growth. They must be able to work as members of multidisciplinary treatment teams and provide holistic behavioral health interventions. Integrated care models hold the promise of addressing many of the challenges facing our health care system. LCMHCs as "primary care providers" are invaluable in developing innovations in integrated public health. These knowledgeable and skilled LCMHCs will be prepared to dramatically reduce the high rates of morbidity and mortality experienced by Americans with mental illness.

1. **Knowledge**

    a. Understand the anatomy and physiology of the brain with particular relevance to mental health.

    b. Gain a working understanding of the most common medical risks and illnesses confronted by patients (e.g., obesity related diseases, substance use disorder related diseases, cardiovascular disease, cancer, diabetes, COPD, etc.)

    c. Understand the processes of stress which relate to impaired immune systems as well as its affects regarding depression and anxiety.

    d. Understand the correlation of trauma, chronic distress, and anxiety with medical health issues, medical diagnoses, medical treatment, and recovery (e.g., post-surgical trauma).

    e. Understand how to triage patients with severe or high-risk behavioral problems to other community resources for specialty mental health services.

    f. Understand and address stressors which lead individuals to seek medical care.

    g. Understand primary (preventing disease) and secondary (coping and ameliorating symptoms) prevention interventions for patients at risk for or with medical and mental health disorders.

    h. Understand and conduct depression, anxiety, and mental health assessments.

    i. Understand and provide cognitive-behavioral interventions.

    j. Understand and assist clients to cope with the medical conditions for which they are receiving medical attention.

    k. Understand and operate in a consultative role within primary care team.

l. Understand and provide recommendations regarding behavioral interventions to referring medical providers.

m. Understand and conduct brief interventions with referred patients on behalf of referring medical providers.

n. Understand the importance of being available for initial patient consultations.

o. Understand the importance of maintaining a visible presence with medical providers during clinic operating hours.

p. Understand and provide a range of services including screening for common conditions, assessments, including risk assessments, and interventions related to chronic disease management programs.

q. Understand and assist in the development of behavioral health interventions (e.g., clinical pathway programs, educational classes, and behavior focused practice protocols).

r. Understand medical concepts needed to effectively function on an integrated health team including these topics and others:
  i. Medical literacy
  ii. Population screening
  iii. Chronic disease management
  iv. Educating medical staff about integrated care
  v. Group interventions
  vi. Evidence-based interventions (See the AMHCA Practice Guideline entitled *Behavioral Health Counseling in Health Care Integration Practices and Health Care System*s)

s. Understand the basic knowledge about key health behaviors and physical health indicators (e.g., normal, risk, and disease level blood chemistry measures) that are routinely assessed and addressed in an integrated system of care, including but not limited to:
  i. Body mass index
  ii. Blood pressure
  iii. Glucose levels
  iv. Lipid levels
  v. Smoking effect on respiration (e.g., carbon monoxide levels)
  vi. Exercise habits
  vii. Nutritional habits
  viii. Substance use frequency (where applicable)
  ix. Alcohol use (where applicable)
  x. Subjective report of physical discomfort, pain or general complaints

t. Understand psychopharmacological treatment of mental health disorders.

Appendix B: *AMHCA Standards for the Practice of Clinical Mental Health Counseling*

2. **Skills**
   a. Demonstrate the ability to understand the dynamics of human development to capture good psychosocial histories of patients.
   b. Diagnose and treat for behavioral pathology.
   c. Provide evidenced-based psychotherapy practices to provide credible treatment to patients.
   d. When appropriate, facilitate and oversee referrals to specialty mental health providers and primary care providers.
   e. Support collaboration of primary care providers with psychiatrists or other prescribing professionals concerning medication protocols.
   f. Monitor psychopharmacological treatment of mental health disorders.
   g. Apply motivational interviewing skills.
   h. Demonstrate consultation liaison skills with other primary care providers.
   i. Provide teaching skills and impart information based on the principles of adult education.
   j. Provide comprehensive integrated screening and assessment skills.
   k. Provide brief behavioral health and substance use intervention and referral skills. Coordinate the treatment of trauma, chronic distress, and anxiety with medical health issues, medical diagnoses, medical treatment, and recovery (e.g., post-surgical trauma).
   l. Provide triage for patients with severe or high-risk behavioral problems to other community resources for specialty mental health services.
   m. Identify and address stressors which lead individuals to seek medical care.
   n. Provide comprehensive care coordination skills.
   o. Provide health promotion, wellness, and whole-health self-management skills in individual and group modalities.
   p. Apply brief interventions using abbreviated evidence-based treatment strategies including, but not limited to:
      i. Solution-focused therapy
      ii. Behavioral activation
      iii. Cognitive behavioral therapy
      iv. Motivational interviewing
   q. Employ behavioral health care techniques to address the needs of geriatric population to address their chronic health issues, disabilities, and deteriorating cognitive needs.
   r. Treat the full spectrum of behavioral health needs, which minimally include:
      i. Common mental health conditions (depression, anxiety)
      ii. Lifestyle behaviors (self-care, social engagement, relaxation, sleep hygiene, diet, exercise, etc.)
      iii. Substance use disorders
   s. Coordinate overall patient care in coordination with the treatment team, including:
      i. Reinforce care plan with other primary care providers

ii. Summarize goals and next steps with patient
t. Lead group sessions for patients (e.g., pain groups, diabetes management, etc.).
u. Provide concise information to the primary care team verbally, through EHR notes, and other appropriate communication channels.

G. Child and Adolescent Standards and Competencies

An estimated one in five youth struggles with mental health challenges. Like adults, children and adolescents struggle with mental disorders that include anxiety, depression, obsessive-compulsive disorder, and post-traumatic stress. Children and adolescents often present different symptomatic presentations of these disorders compared with adults, requiring specialized knowledge of diagnosis and treatment. Several notable neurodevelopmental conditions emerge during early childhood, including autism and spectrum disorders and attention-deficit/ hyperactivity disorder. Late adolescence is also the time when major mental disorders such as bipolar disorder and schizophrenia develop, with prodromal symptoms often appearing earlier in adolescence. The teenage years are a time of experimentation, identity formation and exploration that can have lasting implications throughout the life span (e.g., risk-taking related injuries, substance use and experimentation, sexual experiences, and possible pregnancy).

Licensed Clinical Mental Health Counselors (LCMHCs) can provide more effective services to youth after obtaining knowledge and skill in assessing, diagnosing, and treating these conditions during childhood and adolescence while also remaining informed about developmental neurodevelopmental conditions and other issues that occur during the process of child development.

Treatment approaches to counseling youth can vary substantially, depending on their developmental level and age. For example, younger children do not have the capacity for higher-order cognition and are more likely to benefit from play therapy, and interventions that address parent-child interaction. Mentalization abilities, sometimes referred to as metacognition and theory of mind, develop during adolescence, and this new ability to "think about thinking" provides foundational ability for talk therapy approaches such as cognitive-behavioral therapies, among others.

Early intervention has the potential to improve prognosis of mental disorders over the course of the life span. For example, early behavioral intervention for children with autism spectrum disorders at 2 or 3 years of age can have a greater impact on the acquisition of social skills and language development compared with later remediation. Early intervention with many disorders often yields better prognosis over time.

Family involvement is often a crucial component of treatment for children and adolescents with mental health struggles. Working with parents/guardians to address family dynamics and interactions through family counseling can often facilitate sustained treatment gains and prevent recurrent episodes of symptoms. LCMHCs also need to understand minors' rights in the state that they currently reside, pertinent to the age of consent for adolescents, and parent/guardian rights to see the treatment record. Knowledge and skills pertinent to assessing for child abuse and neglect are also crucial.

LCMHCs working with children and adolescents require specialized culturally competent knowledge and skills pertinent to the inter-related domains of development--cognitive, neurological, physical, sexual, and social development. Additionally, LCMHCs need to understand the educational and academic requirements of P–12 education, the rights and responsibilities of students in their educational systems, the impact of mental health challenges on academic achievement and vice-versa, and study skills required to enhance academic achievement. LCMHCs also need specialized knowledge and skills in working with family systems that support and promote child and adolescent development. An understanding of social influence from peer relationships is also important, particularly during adolescence.

1. **Knowledge**

    LCMHCs must demonstrate knowledge of the following subject areas specific to working with children and adolescents:

    a. Neurophysiological Development
        i. Understand postnatal and infant mental health.
        ii. Understand developmental milestones, transitions, and life span theories relating to children and adolescents.
        iii. Understand neurological brain development during childhood and adolescence, and its impact on executive functioning and decision-making.
        iv. Understand physical and sexual development during childhood and adolescence.
        v. Understand the development of sexual/affective orientation, including the exploration and questioning of sexual and gender identity.

    b. Social, Cultural, and Familial Influences
        i. Understand the role of gender and gender identity on development, including the influence of gender role socialization practices.
        ii. Appreciate sociocultural differences among children and adolescents, including race/ethnicity, acculturation level, family background, and culturally relevant strategies to promote resilience and wellness.
        iii. Understand socioeconomic influences on development, including the impact of poverty, homelessness, and displacement.
        iv. Understand social support system in childhood and adolescence, including family, peer, community, and school-based supports.
        v. Understand the impact of bullying experiences and stigma.
        vi. Understand family relationships, including parent-child relationships, sibling relationships, relationships with extended family, and the impact of domestic violence.
        vii. Understand family events that can generate distress in childhood and adolescence, including parental divorce, and transitions such as stepfamily integration.
        viii. Understand technology and social media use among children and adolescents, including healthy limits with mobile technology use, internet safety, cyber bullying, and appropriate parent/guardian involvement.
        ix. Understand risk factors for externalizing problems such as school truancy, peer influence, substance use, high risk behavior, gang involvement.

    c. Diagnosis and Treatment Planning
        i. Understand risk factors for internalizing problems such as adjustment problems, anxiety, and depression.
        ii. Understand pre-morbid factors associated with the development of severe and persistent mental disorders such as schizophrenia and bipolar disorder.

iii. Understand behaviors associated with neurodevelopmental disorders that include autism, particularly during crucial early developmental period (< 3 years of age).

iv. Understand differential diagnosis for mental disorders that can have similar presentations in children, such as anxiety and attention-deficit/hyperactivity disorders.

v. Understand risk factors for suicide attempts by children and adolescents, and differentiating suicidal from non-suicidal self-injury.

vi. Recognize when referrals are needed for evaluation by a psycho-pharmacologist.

vii. Recognize how psychopharmacological medication prescribing may differ between children/adolescents and adults, such as dosing.

viii. Recognize when consulting with school-based professionals is indicated to inform the treatment process when counseling children and adolescents, including school counselors, psychologists, social workers, teachers, and other school-based mental health professionals.

ix. Understand specialized personality, psychopathology, intelligence, and aptitude assessments for children and adolescents, compared with adults.

x. Understand drug use among children and adolescents, and its impact on development.

d. Academic, Vocational, and Career Development

i. Understand factors associated with academic achievement and underachievement.

ii. Understand school-based legal rights of minors pertinent to special education services and academic accommodations.

iii. Understand career development and vocational aspirations during childhood and adolescence, including early career exploration, influence of social environment on career choice, and impact of school environment on college readiness and vocational training.

e. Legal and Ethical Considerations

i. Understand parent/guardian rights during childhood and adolescence, including minors independently seeking health care services in the U.S. state where the counselor and client reside.

ii. Understand state-based laws pertinent to adolescent emancipation and removal of parental/guardian rights.

iii. Understand physical and emotional signs of child abuse and neglect, interviewing procedures, and appropriate steps required to report such abuse/neglect within timeframes established by state law.

2. **Skills**

LCMHCs must demonstrate skills in the following subject areas specific to working with children and adolescents:

a. Neurophysiological Development

i. Demonstrate the ability to help children and adolescents explore their emerging identity, including cultural, sexual, gender, and vocational identities.

ii. Implement developmentally-appropriate practices when counseling youth, such as using play therapy approaches.

iii. Implement theoretical approaches that are evidence-based practices when counseling child and adolescent clients, not limited to, for example, parent-child interaction therapy, cognitive-behavior therapy, multisystemic family therapy, applied behavior analysis and video modeling (recommended for the care of youth who have autism).

b. Social, Cultural, and Familial Influences

   i. Demonstrate the ability to communicate respectfully and effectively with children, adolescents, and their families, adjusting communication style to match developmental level and considering ethnic, racial, cultural, gender, socioeconomic, and educational backgrounds.

   ii. Demonstrate sensitivity and responsiveness to the child and adolescent's individual and family culture, age, gender, ethnicity, disabilities, socioeconomic background, religious beliefs, and sexual orientation.

   iii. Advocate for the prevention of mental health problems through the creation of social environments in schools and community settings that support optimal mental health and wellness.

   iv. Directly address social problems facing children and adolescents, including intervention related to peer pressure, bullying, gang involvement, and stigmatization.

   v. Support children and adolescents in the aftermath of a crisis, disaster, or other trauma-causing event, including deaths within the local community; prevents contagion of suicidal behavior through public advocacy related to media coverage and responses (e.g., public memorials) of schools and communities.

   vi. Demonstrate the ability to address social problems facing children and adolescents, including bullying, gang involvement, peer pressure, and stigma.

   vii. Demonstrate the ability to strengthen healthy family functioning that impact child and adolescent development, including, inter-parental conflict, domestic violence, parent-child relational problems, parental/guardian over- or under-involvement, authoritarian or passive parenting styles, and addiction in the family.

   viii. Demonstrate ability to address problematic technology and social media use by children and adolescents, including setting healthy limits with mobile technology use, internet safety, cyber bullying, and appropriate parent/guardian involvement.

   ix. Demonstrate an ability to assist youth in the development of face-to-face and technology-based social interaction skills, and address adverse effects of social media dominated communication systems.

c. Diagnosis and Treatment Planning

   i. Demonstrate the ability to assess the various presentations of mental health disorders in children and adolescents, with consideration for developmentally typical and atypical behavior.

   ii. Conduct developmentally appropriate interviewing procedures for assessing suicide risk, homicide risk, and child abuse/neglect.

   iii. Demonstrate ability to assess and treat attachment distress and relational patterns, including attachment-based disorders.

   iv. Demonstrate the ability to plan treatment, including a biopsychosocial formulation, mental status examination, diagnosis, and psychological assessment as it pertains to children and adolescents.

v. Demonstrate familiarity with the diverse micro, meso, and macro systems within the community that are involved in the care of children, adolescents, and their families

vi. Demonstrate the ability to effectively interface with integrated health care professional and collateral sources, enlisting a multidisciplinary approach to the treatment of children and adolescents.

vii. Demonstrate ability to effectively consult with school-based professionals, for example school counselors, psychologists, social workers, teachers, and school-based mental health professionals.

viii. Implement parent education programs and family therapy when indicated.

ix. Implement operant conditioning procedures when appropriate, including behavioral modification and token economy programs.

x. Demonstrate ability to deliver effective psychoeducation to children, adolescents, and families that is matched to developmental level, heeding adaptations designed for adolescents and youth, specifically when available (for example, DBT, CBT, etc.)

xi. Demonstrate ability to form groups that are considerate of developmental level, such as smaller sizes for younger children, and excluding younger children in adolescent groups.

d. Academic, Vocational, and Career Development

i. Demonstrate the ability to assist children and adolescents with strategies (e.g., self-efficacy, planning, organization, etc.) to improve academic performance that is affected by clinical diagnoses and/or concerns, for example autism and spectrum disorder difficulties, ADHD, etc.

e. Legal and Ethical Considerations

Navigate the unique legal challenges related to counseling children, such as age of consent and assent, confidentiality, competence, parental involvement, guardianship, and state laws related to the reporting of child abuse/neglect.

H. Aging and Older Adults Standards and Competencies

Older adults, those aged 60 or above, make important contributions to society as family members, volunteers and as active participants in the workforce. While most have good mental health, many older adults are at risk of developing mental disorders, neurological disorders or substance use problems as well as other health conditions such as diabetes, hearing loss, and osteoarthritis, to name but a few illnesses that may present in older persons. Furthermore, as people age, they are more likely to experience several conditions at the same time.

The key components to successful aging include physical health, mental activity, social engagement, productivity and life satisfaction. When any one of these components are compromised, it can have a negative impact on quality of life. MHC's must understand and address the interaction of these components when working with aging adults.

In addition, older adults are more likely to experience events such as bereavement, a reduction in one's socioeconomic status with retirement, or a disabling condition. All of these factors can result in isolation, loss of independence, loneliness and psychological distress in older adults.

Mental health problems can be under-identified by health care professionals and older adults themselves, and the stigma surrounding mental illness can make older adults reluctant to seek help. Substance use problems among the elderly can also be overlooked or misdiagnosed.

Appendix B: *AMHCA Standards for the Practice of Clinical Mental Health Counseling*

1. **Knowledge**

    LCMHCs in this area of specialization should demonstrate knowledge of the following physical and mental health subject areas specific to working with older adults:

    a. Understand life span developmental theories relating to older adults.

    b. Understand social processes, including topics such as the cultural context of relationships, social engagement and support, leisure and recreation, isolation, productivity (i.e., retirement, loss of identity), sexuality, intimacy, caregiving, self-care, stress relief, abuse and neglect, victimization, and loss and grief.

    c. Understand skills necessary to cope with the emotional and physical challenges associated with the aging process, including how society responds to older adults.

    d. Appreciate psychological aspects of aging, including topics related to the meaning and end of human life according to various religious and cultural viewpoints in relation to topics such as the quality and sacredness of life, end-of-life moral issues, grief and mourning, satisfaction and regret, suicide, and perspectives on life after death.

    e. Recognize and have knowledge of the incidence of suicide among older persons, including warnings signs, risk factors, protective factors, acute vs. chronic risk, the ability to formulate the level of suicidal risk (none, low, moderate, high) using qualified assessment techniques, and managing risk.

    f. Appreciate cultural and ethnic differences among older adults, including culturally relevant strategies to promote resilience and wellness in older adults.

    g. Understand the integration and adjustment of life transitions that occur as part of normal aging (i.e., functional mobility, family constellation, housing, health care, level of care etc.).

    h. Recognize the comorbidity of aging-related and health-related vulnerabilities and strengths.

    i. Recognize the interplay between general medical conditions and mental health, including an understanding of common medications, side effects, drug interactions, and presentation.

    j. Understand drug use and misuse among older adults.

2. **Skills**

    a. Demonstrate the ability to assess the various presentations of mental health disorders (e.g., mood disorders and cognitive and thought disorders, etc.) in older adults and their impact on functional status, morbidity, and mortality.

    b. Demonstrate the ability to communicate respectfully and effectively with older adults and their families, accommodating for hearing, visual, and cognitive deficits.

    c. Demonstrate the ability to communicate respectfully with older adults and their families, recognizing all multicultural considerations unique to older adults, particularly generational values and age-related abilities.

    d. Demonstrate the ability to navigate and address issues associated with the emotional and physical challenges of the aging process, including how society responds to older adults using appropriate counseling strategies.

    e. Demonstrate an ability to navigate the unique challenges related to confidentiality of patient information, informed consent, competence, guardianship, advance directives, wills, and elder abuse.

f. Demonstrate the ability to plan treatment, including a biopsychosocial conceptualization of predisposing, precipitating, and protective factors, mental status evaluation, diagnosis, and mental health assessment as it pertains to older adults.

g. Demonstrate familiarity with the diverse systems of care for patients and their families, and how to use and integrate these resources into a comprehensive treatment plan.

h. Demonstrate the ability to effectively interface with integrated health care professional and collateral sources, enlisting a multidisciplinary approach to the treatment of older adults.

AMHCA Standards for the Practice of Clinical Mental Health Counseling is continually reviewed and updated as appropriate. This unabridged version of the latest *AMHCA Standards* is also downloadable at no cost from *www.amhca.org/publications/standards*.

APPENDIX C

AMHCA CODE OF ETHICS

Ethical Priorities for Clinical Mental Health Counseling

How is the *AMHCA Code of Ethics* distinctive for the profession?

Created by the American Mental Health Counselors Association (AMHCA), the *AMHCA Code of Ethics* focuses on the specific requirements for the ethical practice of Clinical Mental Health Counselors (CMHCs). All recognized professions have codes of ethics to guide the conduct of practice in order to ensure the safety of those served.

As noted throughout "Essentials of the Clinical Mental Health Counseling Profession," the acronym LCMHC is used to refer to all categories of clinical mental health counselors. These categories include Clinical Mental Health Counseling Students (CMHC Students) in supervised internships, postgraduate Supervised Clinical Mental Health Counselors (Supervised CMHCs), and fully Licensed Clinical Mental Health Counselors (LCMHCs).

However, in the *AMHCA Code of Ethics,* the acronym CMHC is used in lieu of LCMHC. CMHC Students, Supervised CMHCs, and LCMHCs all provide mental health counseling services, including the diagnosis and treatment of mental disorders. The *AMHCA Code of Ethics* clarifies that these documents apply to all CMHC Students, Supervised CMHCs, and LCMHCs. Regardless of graduate-degree program title or state license title, *AMHCA Code of Ethics* provides ethical guidelines for each of the clinical mental health counselor categories.

Continuously updated to meet the needs of changing circumstances, the *AMHCA Code of Ethics* addresses the crucial concerns of CMHCs. The association's Ethics Committee, a standing committee, reviews, revises, and adds to the *AMHCA Code of Ethics* in keeping with current standards of practice and applicable ethical standards. This committee serves as a conduit for ethical questions. In this never-ending process, the committee members solicit feedback from CMHCs. They also refer to the codes of ethics in order to be in harmony with the other mental health professions (psychology, social work, and marriage and family therapy). Nevertheless, *AMHCA Code of Ethics* reflects the unique needs of the clinical mental health counseling profession.

With frequent updates, the *Code of Ethics* is often at the forefront of articulating developments in counseling and psychotherapy. For example, technology advances in tele-health (distance counseling) prompted an addition to the *Code of Ethics* to address the concerns of the public and the profession.

AMHCA Code of Ethics has been compared favorably in doctoral research to the codes of ethics of the other mental health professions. It is the most singular discourse regarding ethics for CMHCs.

All members of AMHCA are required to comply with *AMHCA Code of Ethics,* which has been adopted by some states as the standard of ethical practice for CMHCs. Whether or not a CMHC is bound by this *Code of Ethics,* all CMHCs ethically should understand and act in accordance with it. *AMHCA Code of Ethics* is an essential component of practicing clinical mental health counseling with professionalism and integrity. It is required study for AMHCA qualifications and certifications.

In summation, *AMHCA Code of Ethics* offers guidelines for value-directed conduct. While ethical guidance for the practice of clinical mental health counseling is its primary purpose, it is also intended to prompt pondering about ethical thinking and practice. To be an ethical mental health counselor is to practice thinking ethically in an ongoing self-deliberation and in discussions with other mental health professionals.

Using the most frequently asked ethics questions that mental health counselors have submitted, AMHCA's Ethics Committee has compiled the questions and the Committee's answers into an online resource for counselors. Anyone (whether or not a member of AMHCA) can submit a question for consideration. To review the questions and answers, go to "Frequently Asked Questions on Ethics" at *www.amhca.org/publications/ethics/ethicsfaq.*

The unabridged version of *AMHCA Code of Ethics* appears here in Appendix C, and is also available at no cost from *www.amhca.org/publications/ethics.*

AMHCA Code of Ethics (Revised 2020)

Preamble of the AMHCA Code of Ethics

I. Commitment to Clients

- A. Counselor-Client Relationship
    1. Primary Responsibility
    2. Confidentiality
    3. Dual/Multiple Relationships
    4. Exploitive Relationships
    5. Counseling Environments
- B. Counseling Process
    1. Treatment Plans
    2. Informed Consent
    3. Multiple Clients
    4. Clients Served by Others
    5. Termination and Referral
    6. The Use of Technology Supported Counseling and Communications (TSCC)
    7. Clients' Rights
    8. End-of-Life Care for Terminally Ill Clients
- C. Counselor Responsibility and Integrity
    1. Competence
    2. Non-discrimination
    3. Conflict of Interest
- D. Assessment and Diagnosis
    1. Selection and Administration
    2. Interpretation and Reporting
    3. Competence
    4. Forensic Activity
- E. Recordkeeping, Fee Arrangements, and Bartering
    1. Recordkeeping
    2. Fee Arrangements, Bartering, and Gifts

F. Other Roles
   1. Consultant
   2. Advocate

II. Commitment to Other Professionals

   A. Relationship with Colleagues
   B. Clinical Consultation

III. Commitment to Students, Supervisees, and Employee Relationships

   A. Relationships with Students, Interns, and Employees
   B. Commitment for Clinical Supervision
      1. Confidentiality of Clinical Supervision

IV. Commitment to the Profession

   A. Teaching
   B. Research and Publications
   C. Service on Public or Private Boards and Other Organizations

V. Commitment to the Public

   A. Public Statements
   B. Marketing

VI. Resolution of Ethical Problems

Preamble of the *AMHCA Code of Ethics*

The American Mental Health Counselors Association (AMHCA) represents clinical mental health counselors (CMHCs). As the professional association of CMHCs, AMHCA subscribes to rigorous standards for education, training, and clinical practice. CMHCs are committed to increasing knowledge of human behavior and understanding of themselves and others. CMHCs are highly skilled professionals who provide a full range of counseling services in a variety of settings. CMHCs believe in the dignity and worth of the individual and make every reasonable effort to protect human welfare. To this end, AMHCA establishes and promotes the highest professional standards. CMHCs subscribe to and pledge to abide by the principles identified in the *AMHCA Code of Ethics*.

AMHCA Code of Ethics is intended to establish ethical standards for all CMHCs, regardless of AMHCA membership status. The code is a document intended as a guide to assist CMHCs to make sound ethical decisions; to define ethical behaviors and best practices for CMHCs; to support the mission of the association; and to educate members, students and the public at large regarding the ethical standards of CMHCs. CMHCs are expected to utilize carefully considered ethical-decision making processes when faced with ethical dilemmas.

CMHCs are responsible for being aware of federal and state laws, as well as administrative rules and regulations, affecting and governing their practice. In their professional duties, CMHCs may encounter conflicts between the *AMHCA Code of Ethics* and the law, or between local regulatory statute and state law. CMHCs attempt to resolve these conflicts when they occur. When dealing with such conflicts, CMHCs always consider the client's best interest, including continuity of care. When conflicts are unresolvable, CMHCs may adhere to the requirements of the law.

I. Commitment to Clients

A. Counselor-Client Relationship

1. Primary Responsibility

    CMHCs value objectivity and integrity in their commitment to understanding human behavior, and they maintain the highest standards in providing mental health counseling services.

    a. A primary ethical principle of all CMHCs is to ensure client autonomy and self-determination. Therefore, barring cases of imminent harm to self or others, any therapeutic approach that impedes an individual's right to make informed choices is not in accordance with the *AMHCA Code of Ethics*. For specific information regarding conversion therapy, see Appendix D, *AMHCA Statement on Reparative or Conversion Therapy,* on page 141.

    b. CMHCs communicate clearly with clients about the parameters of the counseling relationship. In a professional disclosure statement, they may provide information about expectations and responsibilities of both counselor and client in the counseling process, their professional orientation and values regarding the counseling process, emergency procedures, supervision (as applicable), and business practices.

2. Confidentiality

    CMHCs have an obligation to safeguard information about individuals obtained in the course of practice, teaching, and research. Personal information is communicated to others only with the client's consent, preferably written, or in circumstances dictated by state and federal laws. Disclosure of counseling information is restricted to what is necessary and relevant.

a. Confidentiality is a right granted to all clients of mental health counseling services. From the onset of the counseling relationship, CMHCs inform clients of these rights, including legal limitations and exceptions.

b. The information in client records belongs to the client and shall not be shared without permission granted through a formal release of information. In the event that a client requests that information in client records be shared, CMHCs educate clients to the implications of sharing the materials.

c. The release of information without the consent of the client may only take place under the most extreme circumstances: the protection of life (suicidality or homicidality), child abuse, abuse of persons legally determined as incompetent, and elder abuse. CMHCs are required to comply with state and federal statutes concerning mandated reporting.

d. CMHCs (and their staff members) do not release information by request unless accompanied by a specific release of information or a valid court order. CMHCs make every attempt to release only the information necessary to comply with the request or valid court order. CMHCs are advised to seek legal advice upon receiving a subpoena in order to respond appropriately.

e. The anonymity of clients served in public and other agencies is preserved, if at all possible, by withholding names and personal identifying data. If external conditions require reporting such information, the client shall be so informed.

f. Information received about a client by another agency or person should not be forwarded to another person or agency without the client's written permission.

g. CMHCs have the responsibility to report the validity of data shared with other parties.

h. Case reports presented in classes, professional meetings, and publications shall be disguised so that no identification of the client is possible. Permission must be obtained from clients prior to disclosing their identity.

i. Counseling reports and records are maintained under conditions of security, and provisions are made for their destruction as specified by state regulations. CMHCs ensure that all persons in their employ, as well as volunteers, supervisees and interns, maintain the confidentiality of client information.

j. Sessions with clients may be taped or otherwise recorded only with written permission of the client or guardian. Even with a guardian's written consent, CMHCs should not record a session against the expressed wishes of a client. Such tapes should be destroyed after the timeframe specified by state regulations.

k. The primary client owns the rights to confidentiality. When the primary client is a minor or adult who has been legally determined to be incompetent, parents and guardians have legal access to client information. When appropriate, parent(s) or guardian(s) may be included in the counseling process; however, CMHCs take measures to safeguard client confidentiality within legal limits.

l. In working with families or groups, the rights to confidentiality of each member should be safeguarded. CMHCs make clear that each member of the group has individual rights to confidentiality. CMHCs discuss the limitations to confidentiality.

m. When using a computer to store confidential information, CMHCs control access to such information. As specified by state regulations, the information may be deleted from the system.

n. CMHCs take necessary precautions to ensure client confidentiality of information transmitted electronically through the use of a computer, e-mail, fax, telephone, voice mail, answering machines, or any other electronic means as described in the Telehealth section of this document.

o. CMHCs protect the confidentiality of deceased clients in accordance with legal requirements and agency or organizational policy.

p. CMHCs may disclose information to third-party payers only after clients have authorized such disclosure or as permitted by federal and/or state statute.

3. Dual/Multiple Relationships

CMHCs are aware of their influential position with respect to their clients. CMHCs do not exploit the trust of their clients, nor do they foster client dependency.

a. CMHCs make every effort to avoid dual/multiple relationships with clients that could impair professional judgment or increase the risk of harm. Examples of such relationships may include, but are not limited to, familial, social, financial, business, or close personal relationships with the clients.

b. When deciding whether to enter a dual/multiple relationship with a client, former client, or close relationship to the client, CMHCs will seek consultation and adhere to a credible decision-making process prior to entering this relationship.

c. When a dual/multiple relationship cannot be avoided, CMHCs take appropriate professional precautions such as informed consent, consultation, supervision, and documentation to ensure that judgment is not impaired and that exploitation has not occurred.

d. CMHCs do not accept as clients any individual with whom they are involved in an administrative, supervisory, or other relationship of an evaluative nature.

4. Exploitive Relationships

CMHCs are aware of the intimacy and responsibilities inherent in the counseling relationship. They maintain respect for the client and avoid actions that seek to meet their personal needs at the expense of the client.

a. Romantic or sexual relationships with clients and their immediate family members (i.e., parents, children, and partners) are strictly prohibited. CMHCs do not counsel persons with whom they have had a previous sexual relationship.

b. CMHCs should not knowingly enter into a romantic or sexual relationship with a former client. If a CMHC chooses to enter into such a relationship, the burden to demonstrate that neither coercion nor harm to the client has transpired is on the CMHC and not the former client.

c. Determining the risk of exploitive relationships includes, but is not limited to, factors such as duration of counseling, amount of time since counseling, termination circumstances, the client's personal history and mental status, and the potential adverse impact on the former client.

d. CMHCs are aware of their own values, attitudes, beliefs and behaviors, as well as how these apply in a society with clients from diverse ethnic, social, cultural, religious, and economic backgrounds. CMHCs do not impose their personal values on clients.

5. Counseling Environments

CMHCs will attempt to provide an accessible counseling environment to individuals with disabilities.

a. To the extent possible, counseling environments should be accessible to all clients, including those with disabilities.

b. Counseling environments should allow for private and confidential conversations.

B. Counseling Process

1. Treatment Plans

   CMHCs may use treatment plans to direct their work with clients.

   a. CMHCs and their clients work jointly to devise integrated, individual treatment plans that offer reasonable promise of success and are consistent with the abilities; ethnic, social, cultural, and values backgrounds; and circumstances of the clients.

2. Informed Consent

   Clients have the right to understand what to expect in counseling and the freedom to choose whether and with whom they enter a counseling relationship.

   a. CMHCs provide information that allows clients to make an informed decision about selecting a provider. Such information typically includes counselor credentials, confidentiality protections and limits, the use of tests and inventories, diagnoses, reporting, billing, and therapeutic process. Restrictions that limit clients' autonomy are explained.

   b. When a client is unable to provide consent, CMHCs act in the client's best interest. Parents and legal guardians are informed about the confidential nature of the counseling relationship. CMHCs embrace the diversity of family systems and the inherent rights and responsibilities parents/guardians have for the welfare of their children. CMHCs strive to establish collaborative relationships with parents/guardians to best serve their minor clients.

   c. Informed consent is ongoing and needs to be reassessed throughout the counseling relationship.

   d. CMHCs inform the client of specific limitations, potential risks, and/or potential benefits relevant to the client's anticipated use of online counseling services.

3. Multiple Clients

   When working with multiple clients, CMHCs respect individual client rights and maintain objectivity.

   a. When CMHCs agree to provide counseling services to two or more persons who have a relationship (such as spouses, or parents and children), CMHCs clarify at the outset the nature of the relationship they will have with each involved person.

   b. If it becomes apparent that CMHCs are unable to maintain objectivity, resulting in conflicting roles, they must appropriately clarify, adjust, or withdraw from roles.

   c. Rules of confidentiality extend to all clients who receive services, not just those identified as primary clients.

   d. When working in groups, CMHCs make every effort to screen prospective group counseling participants. Every effort is made to select members whose needs and goals are compatible with goals of the group, who will not impede the group process, and whose well-being will not be jeopardized by the group experience.

Appendix C: *AMHCA Code of Ethics*

   e. In the group counseling setting, CMHCs take reasonable precautions to protect clients from physical, emotional, and psychological harm or trauma.

4. Clients Served by Others

   It is highly recommended that CMHCs should not knowingly enter into counseling relationships with a person being served by another mental health professional, unless all parties have been informed and agree.

   a. When clients choose to change professionals but have not terminated services with the former professional, it is important, if appropriate, to encourage the individual to first deal with that termination prior to entering into a new therapeutic relationship.

   b. When clients work with multiple providers, when appropriate, it is important to secure permission to work collaboratively with the other professional involved.

5. Termination and Referral

   CMHCs do not abandon or neglect their counseling clients.

   a. Assistance is given in making appropriate arrangements for the continuation of treatment, when necessary, during interruptions such as vacation and following termination.

   b. CMHCs may terminate a counseling relationship when it is reasonably clear that the client is no longer benefiting, when services are no longer required, when counseling no longer serves the needs and/or interests of the client, or when agency or institution limits do not allow provision of further counseling services.

   c. CMHCs may terminate a counseling relationship when clients do not pay fees charged or when insurance denies treatment. In such cases, appropriate referrals are offered to the clients.

   d. If CMHCs determine that services are not beneficial to the client, they avoid immediately terminating the counseling relationship. Instead, appropriate referrals are made. If clients decline the suggested referral, CMHCs may discontinue the relationship.

   e. When CMHCs refer clients to other professionals, they will be collaborative.

   f. CMHCs take steps to develop a safety plan if clients are at risk of being harmed or are suicidal. If necessary, they refer to appropriate resources and contact appropriate support.

6. The Use of Technology Supported Counseling and Communications (TSCC)

   CMHCs recognize that technology has become culturally normative worldwide and may employ modern technology communications judiciously, attentive to both the benefits and risks to clients and to the therapeutic process of using technologies to arrange, deliver, or support counseling.

   a. CMHCs understand that the uses of TSCC in counseling may be considered to fall under the following categories:

      i. The use of TSCC as the medium for counseling, also called "telehealth" or "distance counseling," which includes but is not limited to the delivery of counseling by video call (e.g., internet, video chat), by voice (e.g., telephone), by synchronous text (e.g., chat or SMS), or by asynchronous text (e.g., email)

      ii. The use of TSCC as an adjunct to counseling (i.e., for arranging, coordinating, or paying for counseling services), including the use of payment processing services that are integrated with TSCC (e.g. PayPal, Stripe, Zelle) for receipt of payment for counseling services

    iii. The use of online "cloud-based" services for the storage of counseling records

    iv. Marketing, educational forums, and other TSCC to include blogs, webpages, chatroom, etc.

b. CMHCs recognize that federal, state, and local laws prevail and that the standard of care for TSCC is expected in the same manner as face-to-face and in-office counseling. Continuity of care is crucial and, at times, may conflict with local laws and regulations. CMHCs should employ a solid ethical decision-making model to secure continuity of care.

c. CMHCs are not required to provide services via TSCC or may decide not to offer services based on appropriateness.

d. CMHCs only provide telehealth or distance counseling when they have had sufficient training which can be gained through education, supervision, or other appropriate activities (see the TSCC section of *AMHCA Standards for the Practice of Clinical Mental Health Counseling* in Appendix B of the "Essentials of the Clinical Mental Health Counseling Profession" text or online a*t www.amhca.org/publications/standards).*

e. CMHCs need to be familiar with state laws and regulations in both the state in which the CMHC is licensed and the state in which the client is presently located.

f. At the beginning of a course of distance counseling, CMHCs acquire the contact information for emergency services in the location of the client and develop a procedure to follow in the event of a psychiatric or health emergency.

g. In states where there is a legal requirement that CMHCs must include in the client record client communications through TSCC, CMHCs inform the client of that fact.

h. Unless email and text messages are encrypted or otherwise secured or confidential, the client should be informed of the risks and discouraged from using as a means to disclose personal information.

i. Chat Rooms: Typically, unsecured, open chat rooms are discouraged as a platform for communicating with clients.

j. CMHCs may maintain professional profiles that are kept separate from personal profiles. CMHCs need to be aware of their impact on clients should personal information or opinions be disclosed in a public platform. When applicable, CMHCs educate clients on confidentiality, implications for client activity on these pages, and appropriate channels for contacting CMHCs.

k. CMHCs only seek information about their clients through internet searches for the purpose of determining their own or their client's safety, as necessary to conduct a forensic evaluation, or at the client's request.

7. Clients' Rights

Clients have the right to be treated with dignity, consideration, and respect at all times. Clients have the right to:

a. Quality services provided by concerned, trained professionals and competent staff.

b. Confidentiality within the limits of both federal and state law, to be informed about the exceptions to confidentiality, and to expect that no information will be released without the client's knowledge and written consent.

    c. Information such as time of sessions, payment plans/fees, absences, access, emergency procedures, third-party reimbursement procedures, termination and referral procedures, and advanced notice of the use of collection agencies.

    d. Clear information about the purposes and goals of counseling.

    e. Appropriate information regarding the CMHC's education, training, and practice limitations.

    f. Full, knowledgeable, and responsible participation in the ongoing treatment plan to the maximum extent feasible.

    g. Obtain information about their case record and to have this information explained clearly and directly.

    h. Request information and/or consultation regarding the progress of their therapy.

    i. Refuse any recommended services, techniques, or approaches and to be advised of the consequences of this action.

    j. A safe environment for counseling free of emotional, physical, or sexual abuse.

    k. A clearly defined termination process, and to discontinue therapy at any time.

8. End-of-Life Care for Terminally Ill Clients

    a. CMHCs ensure that clients receive quality end-of-life care for their physical, emotional, social, and spiritual needs. This includes providing clients with an opportunity to participate in informed decision-making regarding their end-of-life care, and a thorough assessment from a qualified professional of clients' ability to make competent decisions on their behalf.

    b. CMHCs are aware of their own competency as it relates to end-of-life decisions. When CMHCs assess that they are unable to work with clients on the exploration of end-of-life options, they make appropriate referrals to ensure clients receive appropriate help.

    c. Depending on the applicable state laws, the circumstances of the situation, and after seeking consultation and supervision from competent professional and legal entities, CMHCs have the option to respect the confidentiality of terminally ill clients who plan to end their lives.

C. Counselor Responsibility and Integrity

1. Competence

    The maintenance of high standards of professional competence is a responsibility shared by all CMHCs in the best interests of the client, the public, and the profession. CMHCs:

    a. Recognize the boundaries of their particular competencies and the limitations of their expertise.

    b. Provide only those services and use only those techniques for which they are qualified by education, training, or experience.

    c. Maintain knowledge of relevant scientific and professional information related to the services rendered and recognize the need for ongoing education.

    d. Represent accurately their competence, education, training, and experience including licenses and certifications.

    e. Perform their duties as teaching professionals based on careful preparation, so that their instruction is accurate and educational.

f. Recognize the importance of continuing education and remain open to new counseling approaches and procedures documented by peer-reviewed scientific and professional literature.

g. Recognize the important need to be competent with respect to cultural diversity; CMHCs are sensitive to the diversity of different populations and to changes in cultural expectations and values over time.

h. Recognize that their effectiveness is dependent on their own mental and physical health. Should their professional judgment or competency be compromised for any reason, they seek capable professional assistance to determine whether to limit, suspend, or terminate services to their clients.

i. Have a responsibility to maintain high standards of professional conduct at all times.

j. Take appropriate steps to informally resolve ethical issues with colleagues, when appropriate, by bringing concerns to their attention. When informal resolution is inappropriate, CMHCs may pursue more formal options, such as state licensing boards.

k. Have a responsibility to empower clients, when appropriate.

l. Are aware of the intimacy of the counseling relationship, maintain a healthy respect for the integrity of the client, and avoid engaging in activities that seek to meet the CMHC's personal needs at the expense of the client.

m. Actively attempt to understand the diverse cultural backgrounds of the clients with whom they work. This includes learning how the CMHC's own cultural/ethical/racial/religious identities impact their own values and beliefs about the counseling process.

n. Are responsible for continuing education and remaining abreast of current trends and changes in the field, including the professional literature on best practices.

o. Develop a plan for termination of practice, death, or incapacitation by assigning a colleague or records custodian to handle transfer of clients and files.

p. Make an effort to avoid using language that may be offensive to individuals.

2. Non-Discrimination

a. CMHCs do not condone or engage in discrimination based on ability status, age, culture, ethnicity, sex, gender identity, race, religion, national origin, political beliefs, sexual orientation, relationship status, or socioeconomic status.

b. CMHCs do not condone or engage in sexual harassment.

c. CMHCs have a responsibility to educate themselves about their own biases toward those of different races, creeds, identities, orientations, cultures, and physical and mental abilities, and then to seek consultation, supervision, and/or counseling in order to prevent those biases from interfering with the counseling process.

3. Conflict of Interest

a. CMHCs are aware of possible conflicts of interest that may arise among counselors, employers, consultants, and other professionals.

b. CMHCs may choose to consult with any other professionally competent person about a client, assuring that no conflict of interest exists. When conflicts occur, CMHCs clarify the nature of the conflict, inform all parties of the nature of their loyalties and responsibilities, and keep all parties informed of their commitments.

D. Assessment and Diagnosis

1. Selection and Administration

    CMHCs utilize educational, psychological, diagnostic, and career assessment instruments (herein referenced as "tests"), interviews, and other assessment techniques and diagnostic tools in the counseling process for the purpose of determining the client's particular needs.

    a. CMHCs choose assessment methods that are reliable, valid, and appropriate based on their client's age, gender, race, ability status, etc. If tests must be used in the absence of information regarding the aforementioned factors, the limitations of generalizability should be duly noted.

    b. In selecting assessment tools, CMHCs justify the logic of their choices in relation to the client's needs and the clinical context in which the assessment occurs.

    c. CMHCs avoid using outdated or obsolete tests and remain current regarding test publications and revisions.

    d. CMHCs use assessments only in the context of professional, academic, or training relationships.

    e. CMHCs provide the client with appropriate information regarding the reason for the assessment and to whom the report will be distributed.

    f. CMHCs provide an appropriate assessment environment.

2. Interpretation and Reporting

    CMHCs respects the rights and dignity of the client in assessment, interpretation, and diagnosis of mental disorders and make every effort to assure that the client receives appropriate treatment.

    a. CMHCs base their diagnoses and other assessment summaries on multiple sources of data whenever possible.

    b. CMHCs consider multicultural factors in test interpretation, diagnosis, and the formulation of prognosis and treatment recommendations.

    c. CMHCs are responsible for evaluating the quality of computer software interpretations of test data. CMHCs should obtain information regarding the validity of computerized test interpretation before utilizing such an approach.

    d. CMHCs clearly explain test results in their summaries and reports.

    e. CMHCs write reports in a style that is clear, concise, and understandable for the lay reader.

    f. CMHCs provide test results in a neutral and nonjudgmental manner.

    g. CMHCs are responsible for ensuring the confidentiality and security of assessment reports, test data, and test materials regardless of how the material is maintained or transmitted.

    h. CMHCs train their staff to respect the confidentiality of test reports.

    i. CMHCs and their staff members do not release an assessment or evaluation report by request unless accompanied by a specific release of information or a valid court order. By itself, a subpoena may be an insufficient reason to release a report. In such a case, the counselor should inform the client of the situation. If the client refuses release, the CMHC coordinates between the client's attorney and the requesting attorney to protect client confidentiality and the counselor's legal welfare.

3. Competence

    CMHCs employ only those diagnostic tools and assessment instruments they are trained to use by education or supervised training and clinical experience.

    a. CMHCs seek appropriate workshops, supervision, and training to familiarize themselves with assessment techniques and the use of specific assessment instruments.

    b. CMHC supervisors ensure that their supervisees have adequate training in interpretation before allowing them to evaluate tests independently.

4. Forensic Activity

    CMHCs who are requested or required to perform forensic functions such as assessments, interviews, consultations, report writing, responding to subpoenas, or offering expert testimony comply with the provisions of the *AMHCA Code of Ethics* and act in accordance with applicable state and federal law.

    a. CMHCs who engage in forensic activity are expected to possess appropriate knowledge and competence.

    b. When conducting interviews, writing reports, or offering testimony, CMHCs objectively offer their findings without bias or investment in the ultimate outcome.

    c. CMHCs inform clients involved in a forensic evaluation about the limits of confidentiality, the role of the CMHC, and the purpose of the assessment.

    d. CMHCs' written forensic reports and recommendations are based on information and techniques appropriate to the evaluation.

    e. CMHCs do not provide written conclusions or forensic testimony regarding any individual without assessment of that individual adequate to support statements and conclusions offered in the forensic setting.

    f. When testifying, CMHCs clearly present their qualifications and specialized training. They accurately describe the basis for their professional judgment, conclusions, and testimony.

    g. CMHCs do not typically provide forensic evaluations for individuals whom they are currently counseling or have counseled in the past. Conversely, CMHCs do not typically counsel individuals they are currently evaluating, or have evaluated in the past, for forensic purposes.

    h. Forensic CMHCs do not act as an advocate for the legal system, perpetrators, or victims of criminal activity.

E. Record-Keeping, Fee Arrangements, and Bartering

1. Recordkeeping

    CMHCs create and maintain accurate and adequate clinical and financial records.

    a. CMHCs create, maintain, store, transfer, and dispose of client records in ways that protect confidentiality and are in accordance with applicable regulations or laws.

    b. CMHCs establish a plan for the transfer, storage, and disposal of client records in the event of withdrawal from practice or death of the counselor in a manner that maintains confidentiality and protects the welfare of the client.

c. When CMHCs choose to exceed state minimum requirements for maintaining records, they must notify clients in their informed consent.

d. All communication regarding mental health treatment, including emails and texts, should be kept.

2. Fee Arrangements, Bartering, and Gifts

CMHCs are cognizant of cultural norms in relation to fee arrangements, bartering, and gifts. CMHCs clearly explain to clients, early in the counseling relationship, all financial arrangements related to counseling.

a. CMHCs usually refrain from accepting goods or services from clients in return for counseling services, because such arrangements may create the potential for conflicts, exploitation, and distortion of the professional relationship. However, bartering may occur if the client requests it, there is no exploitation, and the cultural implications and other concerns of such practice are discussed with the client and agreed on in writing.

b. CMHCs are encouraged to contribute to society by providing pro bono, volunteer, or reduced rate/sliding scale services when feasible.

c. When accepting gifts, CMHCs take into consideration the therapeutic relationship, motivation of giving, the counselor's motivation for receiving or declining, cultural norms, and the value of the gift.

F. Other Roles

1. Consultant

CMHCs, when in a consulting role, have a high degree of self-awareness of their own values, knowledge, skills, and needs in entering a helping relationship that involves human and/or organizational change.

a. The focus of the consulting relationship is on the issues to be resolved and not on the personal characteristics of those presenting the consulting issues.

b. CMHCs develop an understanding of the problem presented by the client and secure an agreement with the client, specifying the terms and nature of the consulting relationship.

c. CMHCs ensure, whenever feasible, that they and their clients have the competencies and resources necessary to follow the consultation plan.

d. CMHCs encourage adaptability and growth toward self-direction.

e. CMHCs keep all proprietary and client information confidential.

f. CMHCs avoid conflicts of interest in selecting consultation clients.

2. Advocate

CMHCs are encouraged to advocate at the individual, institutional, professional, and societal level to foster sociopolitical change that advances client and community welfare.

a. CMHCs are aware of and make every effort to avoid pitfalls of advocacy including conflicts of interest, inappropriate relationships, and other negative consequences. CMHCs remain sensitive to the potential personal and cultural impact on clients of their advocacy efforts.

b. CMHCs may encourage clients to challenge familial, institutional, and societal obstacles to their growth and development and they may advocate on the clients' behalf. CMHCs remain aware of the potential dangers of becoming overly involved as an advocate.

c. CMHCs generally speak only on their own behalf. When authorized to speak on the behalf of a counseling organization, they make every effort to be clear and cautious in their communication, accurately portraying the position of the authorizing organization.

d. CMHCs endeavor to speak factually and discern facts from opinions.

II. Commitment to Other Professionals

A. Relationship with Colleagues

1. CMHCs treat colleagues and other professionals with respect.

2. CMHCs understand how related professions complement their work and make full use of other professional, technical, and administrative resources that best serve the interests of clients.

3. CMHCs treat professional colleagues with dignity and respect. Professional discourse should be free of personal attacks. CMHC recognize and respect professional cultural differences.

4. CMHCs respect the viability, reputation, and proprietary rights of organizations that they serve.

5. Credit is assigned to those who have contributed to a publication in proportion to their contribution.

6. CMHCs do not accept or offer referral fees from other professionals.

7. When CMHCs have knowledge of the impairment, incompetence, or unethical conduct of a mental health professional, they are expected to attempt to rectify the situation. Failing an informal resolution, CMHCs should bring such unethical activities to the attention of the appropriate state licensing board and/or the ethics committee of the professional association.

B. Clinical Consultation

CMHCs may offer or seek clinical consultation from other mental health professionals. In clinical consultation, CMHCs provide critical and supportive feedback. Clinical consultation does not imply hierarchy or responsibility for client outcome.

III. Commitment to Students, Supervisees, and Employee Relationships

A. Relationships with Students, Interns, and Employees

CMHCs respect the integrity and welfare of supervisees, students, and employees. These relationships typically include an evaluative component and therefore need to be maintained on a professional and confidential basis. For more information about supervision disclosure, please see Appendix E, *AMHCA Clinical Supervision Disclosure Template,* on page 143.

1. CMHCs recognize the influential position they have with regard to both current and former supervisees, students, and employees and avoid exploiting their trust and dependency.

2. CMHCs do not engage in ongoing counseling relationships with current supervisees, students, and employees.

3. Sexual behavior with supervisees, students, and employees is unethical.

4. CMHCs do not engage in harassment of supervisees, students, employees, or colleagues.

5. CMHC supervisors ensure that their supervisees, students, and employees accurately represent their training, experience, and credentials.

6. In the informed consent statement, students and supervisees notify the client that they are in supervision and provide their clients with the name and credentials of their supervisor.

7. Students and supervisees have the same ethical obligations to clients as those required of CMHCs.

8. Supervisors should provide written informed consent prior to beginning a supervision relationship.

B. Commitment for Clinical Supervision

Clinical supervision is an important component of the counseling process. Supervision assists the supervisee to provide the best treatment possible to counseling clients and to provide training to the supervisee, which is an integral part of counselor education. Supervision also serves a gatekeeping process to ensure safety to the client, the profession, and to the supervisee.

1. Confidentiality of Clinical Supervision

    Clinical supervision is a part of the treatment process, and therefore all of the clinical information shared between a supervisee and supervisor is confidential. Clinical supervisors do not disclose client information except:

    a. To prevent clear and imminent danger to a person or persons

    b. As mandated by law for child or senior abuse reporting

    c. When there is a written waiver of confidentiality obtained prior to such a release of information

    d. When the release of records or information is permitted by state or federal law

    e. In educational or training settings when information has effectively been deidentified or when written permission has been obtained from the client

IV. Commitment to the Profession

CMHCs promote the mission, goals, values, and knowledge of the profession. They engage in activities that maintain and increase the respect, integrity, and knowledge base of the counseling profession and human welfare. Such activities include but are not limited to teaching, research, serving on professional boards, and membership in professional associations.

A. Teaching

As teaching professionals, CMHCs perform their duties based on careful preparation to provide instruction that is accurate, current, and educational.

B. **Research and Publications**

As researchers, CMHCs conduct investigations and publish findings with respect for the dignity and welfare of the participants and integrity of the profession.

1. The ethical researcher seeks advice from other professionals if any plan of research suggests a deviation from any ethical principle of research with human participants. Such deviation protects the dignity and welfare of the client and places on the researcher a special burden to act in the participant's interest.

2. The ethical researcher is open and honest in the relationship with research participants.

3. The ethical researcher protects participants from physical and mental discomfort, harm, and danger. If the risks of such consequences exist, the investigator is required to inform participants of that fact, secure consent before proceeding, and take all possible measures to minimize the distress.

4. The ethical researcher instructs research participants that they are free to withdraw from participation at any time.

5. The ethical researcher understands that information obtained about research participants during the course of an investigation is confidential. When the possibility exists that others may obtain access to such information, participants are made aware of the possibility and the plan for protecting confidentiality and for storage and disposal of research records.

6. The ethical researcher gives sponsoring agencies, host institutions, and publication channels the same respect and opportunity for informed consent that they accord to individual research participants.

7. The ethical researcher is aware of the obligation to future research and ensures that host institutions are given feedback and proper acknowledgement.

C. **Service on Public or Private Boards and Other Organizations**

When serving as members of governmental or other organizational bodies, CMHCs represent the counseling profession and are accountable as individuals to the *Code of Ethics* of the American Mental Health Counselors Association.

V. Commitment to the Public

CMHCs recognize they have a moral, legal, and ethical responsibility to the community and to the general public. CMHCs are aware of the prevailing community and cultural values, and the impact of professional standards on the community.

A. **Public Statements**

In their professional roles, CMHCs may be expected or required to make public statements providing counseling information or professional opinions, or supply information about the availability of counseling products and services. CMHCs accurately represent their education, professional qualifications, licenses, and credentials. Public statements serve the purpose of providing information to aid the public in making informed judgments and choices. Public statements will be consistent with this *AMHCA Code of Ethics*.

B. Marketing

When advertising or promoting their professional services, CMHCs include only information that is accurate.

VI. Resolution of Ethical Problems

AMHCA members are encouraged to consult with the AMHCA Ethics Committee regarding processes to resolve ethical dilemmas that may arise in clinical practice. Members are also encouraged to use commonly recognized procedures for ethical decision-making to resolve ethical conflicts. For an example of an ethical decision-making model, see Appendix F, *The AMHCA Ethical Decision-Making Model,* on page 147.

The American Mental Health Counselors Association, its board of directors, and its national Committee on Ethics do not investigate or adjudicate ethical complaints. In the event a member has his or her license suspended or revoked by an appropriate state licensure board, the AMHCA board of directors may then act in accordance with AMHCA's by-laws to suspend or revoke his or her membership.

Any member so suspended may apply for reinstatement upon the reinstatement of his or her licensure.

See related appendixes for supporting documentation regarding the following topics:

- *AMHCA Statement on Reparative or Conversion Therapy* (Appendix D on page 141)
- *Clinical Supervision Disclosure Template* (Appendix E on page 143)
- *The AMHCA Ethical Decision-Making Model* (Appendix F on page 147)

Download the *AMHCA Code of Ethics* at no cost from *www.amhca.org/publications/ethics*.

APPENDIX D

AMHCA Statement on Reparative or Conversion Therapy

Adopted by the AMHCA board of directors, July 10, 2014, Alexandria, VA

"Reparative" or "conversion" therapy, are practices by mental health providers that seek to change an individual's sexual orientation or gender identity. These practices include efforts to change behaviors or to eliminate or reduce sexual or romantic attractions and/or feelings toward individuals of the same sex.

Reparative therapy does not include psychotherapies that aim to provide acceptance, support, and understanding of clients or the facilitation of clients' coping, social support, and identity exploration and development including sexual orientation-neutral interventions to prevent or address unlawful conduct or unsafe sexual practices. Nor does reparative therapy include counseling for a person seeking to transition from one gender to another.

There is virtually no credible evidence that any type of psychotherapy can change a person's sexual orientation, gender identity or expression, and, in fact, these efforts pose critical health risks to lesbian, gay, bisexual, and transgender people, including depression, shame, decreased self-esteem, social withdrawal, substance use, risky behavior, and suicidality.

As mental health advocates, AMHCA knows that sexual and gender minorities seeking therapy can benefit from interventions that reduce and counter internalized stigma and increase active coping.

We are concerned that reparative therapy has been documented to do exactly the opposite by increasing internalized stigma and potentially resulting in numerous negative side effects. Additionally, some treatment programs using reparative therapy may provide inaccurate scientific information on sexual orientation and/or gender identity, and may be fear-based, again with the potential to increase distress in treatment participants. Moreover, reparative therapy is scientifically flawed since it is based on the notion that homosexuality is not a normal sexual expression.

AMHCA recommends that counseling around sexual orientation or gender identity follows the framework of an "affirmative therapeutic intervention." This approach means that the therapist addresses the stress-inducing stigma experienced by sexual and gender minorities with interventions designed to reduce that stress, including helping the client overcome negative attitudes about themselves.

Reparative therapy reinforces negative attitudes about sexual minority status and has been shown to increase stress by reaffirming stigma.

Existing law provides for licensing and regulation of various mental health professionals. Additionally, many state laws already prohibit certain types of controversial psychological therapies, including psychosurgery, convulsive therapy, and experimental treatments or behavior modification programs that involve aversive stimuli or deprivation of rights.

AMHCA supports initiatives that will curb harmful practices that have documented iatrogenic effects and will thus help ensure the overall health and safety of LGBT youth.

[For clarification, "iatrogenic" is defined by Merriam-Webster as "induced inadvertently by a physician or surgeon or by medical treatment or diagnostic procedures."]

APPENDIX E

AMHCA Clinical Supervision Disclosure Template

Supervisors provide informed consent/contract prior to beginning a supervision relationship that documents but is not limited to:

- ❏ Business address
- ❏ Telephone number and other contact information
- ❏ List of degrees, license, and credentials/certifications held
- ❏ Areas of competence in clinical mental health counseling
- ❏ Training in supervision and experience providing supervision
- ❏ Model of or approach to supervision, including the role of the supervisor and the objectives, and modalities of supervision
- ❏ Evaluation procedures in the supervisory relationship
- ❏ The limits and scope of confidentiality and privileged communication within the supervisory relationship
- ❏ Procedures for supervisory emergencies and supervisor absences
- ❏ Use of supervision agreements
- ❏ Procedures for supervisee endorsement for certification and/or licensure, or employment to those whom are competent, ethical, and qualified
- ❏ Fees for group and individual services
- ❏ The records to be maintained by both supervisor and supervisee regarding issues discussed in supervision, the number of hours of supervision, and whether the supervision was individual or group format
- ❏ The agreement of supervisor and supervisee regarding how often the supervision sessions will be scheduled and the frequency of supervision sessions, which shall comply with state regulations
- ❏ Signature and date

In addition to the recommended contract, the following practice guidelines for clinical supervision should be communicated between supervisors and supervisees:

a. *Insurance.* The supervisee will maintain a professional liability insurance policy during the clinical supervision process and will provide a copy of a certificate of insurance to the supervisor.

b. *Compliance with AMHCA Code of Ethics.* The supervisor should provide a copy of *AMHCA Code of Ethics* to the supervisee, or ensure that the supervisee has obtained a copy of *AMHCA Code of Ethics*. The supervisee must agree to comply with the *AMHCA Code of Ethics* in all treatment provided. As needed, the supervisor and supervisee will discuss the principles contained in *AMHCA Code of Ethics*. The supervisor needs to be aware of other codes of ethics that may apply to the supervisee.

c. *State Licensing Board Rules.* The supervisee needs to obtain a copy of the appropriate state licensing body rules (or know how to access the rules online) and agree to comply with them. As needed, the supervisor and supervisee will discuss the provisions of board rules. The supervisor will be aware of all credentials and membership organizations regulating the supervisee.

d. *Compliance with State Laws.* The supervisor should inform the supervisee of state laws governing the practice of CMHCs and other legal provisions that apply to treatment, requirements for licensure, billing, and the discipline of counselors.

e. *Duty of the Clinical Supervisor.* The contract should specify that the duty of the clinical supervisor will be to direct the treatment process, and to assist the supervisee in complying with all legal and ethical standards for treatment.

f. *Billing for Treatment.* Supervisee should agree that all bills submitted for treatment will accurately reflect the amount of time spent in counseling session and will also identify the professional who provided services to the client.

g. *Treatment Records and Bills.* As part of the supervision process, the supervisee will agree to provide treatment records and billing statements to the clinical supervisor on request. In addition, the supervisee will agree to maintain all treatment records securely, to maintain their confidentiality and to comply with state recordkeeping requirements.

h. *Informed Consent.* The supervisee will agree to obtain informed consent in writing from the counseling client in compliance with state law. In addition, the supervisee will obtain informed consent in writing from any client whose treatment session is to be videotaped, recorded, or observed through one-way glass.

i. *Dual Relationships.* Supervisors will avoid all dual relationships that may interfere with the supervisor's professional judgment or exploit the supervisee. Any sexual, romantic, or intimate relationship is considered to be a violation. Sexual relationship means sexual conduct, sexual harassment, or sexual bias toward a supervisee by a supervisor.

j. *Termination of Supervision.* When a supervisee discontinues supervision, a written notice that the supervision process has terminated should be provided by the supervisor, along with an appropriate referral for supervision. If during supervision a conflict arises which causes impairment to the professional judgment of the supervisor or supervisee, the process should be terminated and a referral made. Both the supervisor and the supervisee have the right to terminate supervision at any time, with reasonable notice being provided regarding the voluntary termination of supervision.

k. *Consultation for the Supervisor.* Whenever a clinical supervisor needs to discuss questions regarding the clinical services being provided, ethical issues, or legal matters, the supervisor should obtain a consultation in order to resolve the issue. That consultation must be documented in the supervisor's clinical supervision notes.

Appendix E: *AMHCA Clinical Supervision Disclosure Template*

l. *Credentials for Supervisors.* A supervisor should have the level of clinical experience required by state regulations, which is required for supervision of other professionals. In addition, the supervisor should have training in the clinical supervision process.

m. *Credentials for Supervisees.* Supervisors must ensure that supervisees have the requisite credentials under state law to provide counseling to clients. If at any time during the supervision process a supervisor concludes that the supervisee does not have the requisite skills and education to provide counseling safely, and the supervisee is not showing evidence of learning or progressing, the supervisor should inform the supervisee of the deficiencies noted in the supervisor's evaluation of the supervisee, and terminate the relationship.

OPTIONAL: Supervisors may communicate expectations regarding the participation in professional associations and activities related to professional identity and professional advocacy.

APPENDIX F

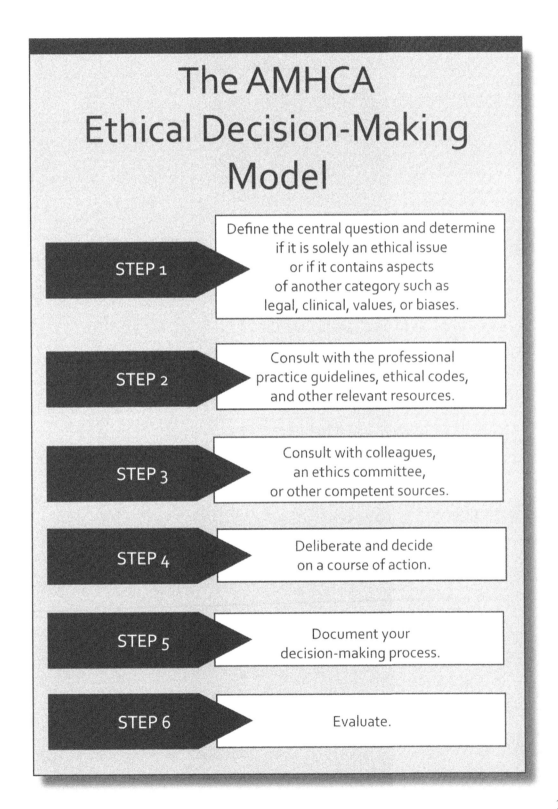

APPENDIX G

The Clinical Mental Health Counselor Declaration: A Hippocratic Pledge

See the next page for a copy of *The AMHCA Declaration* suitable for framing or distribution, or visit *www.amhca.org/publications/declaration*.

The Clinical Mental Health Counselor Declaration
A Hippocratic Pledge

Clinical Mental Health Counselors advocate for the well-being of individuals, families, and communities. They are highly trained and qualified to provide comprehensive assessment, diagnosis, and treatment of mental health disorders as well as barriers to quality of life. Members of the profession also integrate mental health with social, cultural, vocational, educational, and physical wellness.

As a Clinical Mental Health Counselor:

I pledge to dedicate my professional life to the service of humanity;

My first consideration will be to improve the mental, emotional, and relational well-being of those within my care, their families, and the community at large;

I will engage in my profession with integrity and in keeping with codes of ethics, laws, and the best practices of Clinical Mental Health Counseling;

I will maintain the utmost respect for each individual and will honor their autonomy, dignity, and self-determination;

I will respect the confidences that are disclosed to me, in accordance with relevant laws and codes of ethics;

I will recognize and address presumptions related to gender, age, race, ethnic origin, sexual orientation, disease, ability level, creed, nationality, or any other factors so they will not interfere with my duties;

I will honor my professional capabilities, so that even under threat, I will not violate human rights or civil liberties;

I will share my professional knowledge and work in partnership with other health professionals;

I will extend fitting respect and gratitude to my teachers, colleagues, and students;

I will use my knowledge, skills, and experiences to prepare the next generation of Clinical Mental Health Counselors;

I will attend to my own well-being, my physical wellness, and my personal relationships;

I will accept my lifelong obligation to improve my professional capabilities in order to provide the highest standard of care; and

As a Clinical Mental Health Counselor, I will advocate for the betterment of others and for the advancement of health and well-being.

I make this declaration solemnly, freely, and on my honor.

END NOTE

"Essentials of the Clinical Mental Health Counseling Profession"
is a living document that AMHCA will update regularly.

Readers are encouraged to contribute ideas for future updates
by using the comment box on the "Essentials" page at *www.amhca.org/publications/essentials*.

Online updates will be available on *www.amhca.org/publications/essentials* in between printed editions.

"Essentials" is a reflection of the contributions of many AMHCA members.
All of us who are members of the profession of clinical mental health counseling
stand on the shoulders of those who have gone before us. These individuals
founded and sustained AMHCA and this distinctive profession,
which has made such a profound difference for so many.

Made in the USA
Coppell, TX
11 July 2021